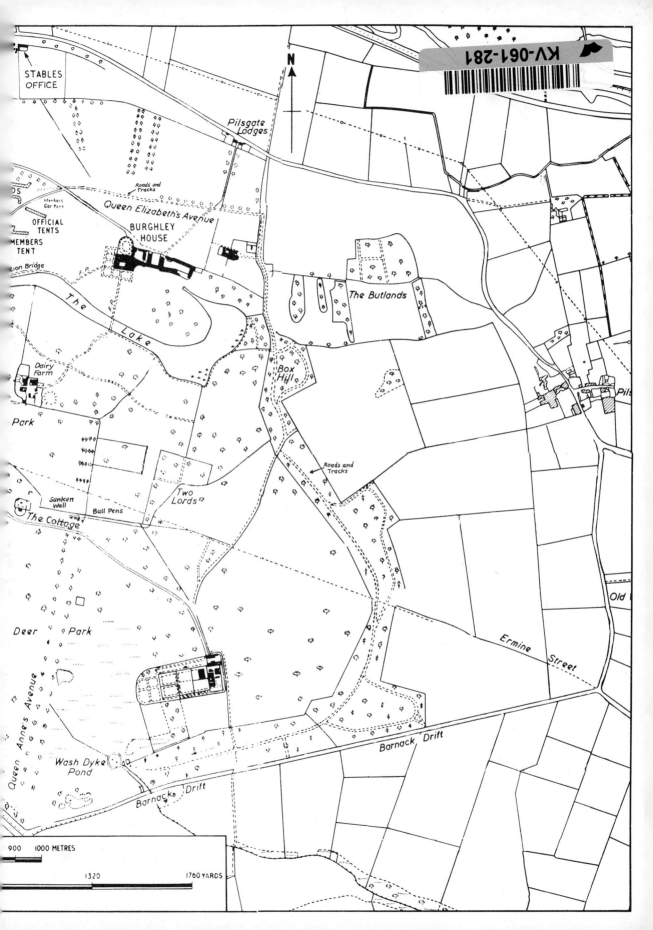

STABLES
OFFICE

N

Pilsgate
Lodges

Roads and
Tracks

Members
Car Park

Queen Elizabeth's Avenue

OFFICIAL
TENTS

BURGHLEY
HOUSE

MEMBERS
TENT

The Butlands

Lion Bridge

F.P.

The Lake

Box
Hill

Dairy
Farm

Park

Roads and
Tracks

Two
Lords

Sunken
Wall

Bull Pens

The Cottage

Deer   Park

Ermine   Street

Old

Queen Anne's Avenue

Wash Dyke
Pond

Barnack Drift

Barnack   Drift

Pils

900   1000 METRES

1320

1760 YARDS

BURGHLEY
The Three-Day Event

BURGHLEY
The Three-Day Event

**Foreword
by
Her Royal Highness
The Princess Anne**

**Threshold Books Limited
London**

Devised and written (except chapters 2, 4, 5 & 6)
by **Anna Buxton**

Designed by Jonathan Gill-Skelton

Picture research by Marian L. Eason

Filmset in 'Monophoto' Plantin 11 on 12 pt. by
Richard Clay (The Chaucer Press), Ltd., Bungay, Suffolk
and printed in Great Britain by
Fletcher & Son Ltd., Norwich

Published by Threshold Books Limited
200 Buckingham Palace Road
London SW1

ISBN 0 90136601 3

*Jacket illustration: View of Burghley House during the
World Championships in 1974.*

*Frontispiece: Burghley, 1971. Princess Anne, winner
of the European Individual Championship, is
congratulated by The Queen and Prince Philip after the
presentation of the trophy.*

Contents

Acknowledgements

I would like to thank the Marquess of Exeter for allowing me to undertake this book and for telling me about his house and family; Sir Giles Floyd for showing me round the house and for answering innumerable questions; and Dr Till for reading the manuscript of the first chapter. I would also like to express gratitude to Brigadier James Grose and to Bill Thomson for providing a good deal of the information for Chapters 2 and 3 respectively. Edna Stokes and the staff in the office at Burghley have generously given us their time and help. Major Andrew Burnaby-Atkins, who was Trials Director when I first had the idea for the book, gave me the go-ahead, and Charles Stratton, the present Director, endorsed his support. Raleigh Industries, the sponsors of the Event, have also been most helpful and encouraging.

Denny Emerson's fence-by-fence account of his round in 1974 first appeared in the United States Combined Training Association's News and we are grateful to the USCTA for permission to reprint it. I would also like to thank all the competitors who have dug deep into their memories for my benefit, and Alan Smith for lending me his cuttings. My husband's contribution has been incalculable. Without Barbara Cooper, the publisher, this book would not have been possible.

Anna Buxton, London, 1978

Foreword

BUCKINGHAM PALACE

It all seems a long time ago now - that really beautiful autumn weekend in 1971. I had never been to Burghley before and I stayed in that Elizabethan palace of a house which is itself a quite intimidating experience. It was my second major Three Day Event and only my third ever, so to say that I was feeling apprehensive would be no exaggeration!

What happened is now history, but needless to say Burghley now holds a rather special place in my memory and I tend to judge each course that has been built since against the one that I won over. A purely personal point of view of course and I am grateful to Anna Buxton and this book for allowing me to relive those nerve racking days and to read how others felt when they achieved victory in the lovely grounds of Burghley.

Anne

CHAPTER I

Burghley and the Cecils

Burghley House, magnificent four-hundred-year-old palace of the Cecil family, stands massive and serene, remote from the bustle of the horse trials. From a distance it is the fantastic roof-line that catches the eye, with its profusion of tall chimneys disguised as Doric columns, its spiked cupolas and octagonal domes, the obelisk of the clock tower in the court-yard, and the fretwork of the balustrade. Architecturally it is one of England's most important Elizabethan buildings—with its exterior, apart from the south front, little changed since it was completed in 1587. Inside it contains not only one of the best private collections of Italian paintings, but also in the late seventeenth-century state rooms and private apartments some of England's finest Baroque decoration. All this a family home set in Capability Brown's elegant eighteenth-century landscape.

It is a setting that seems entirely appropriate for the arduous sport of Three-Day Eventing, which for all its modernity seems to have evolved from so many strands in the English equestrian tradition. Here David Brownlow, 6th Marquess and 15th Earl of Exeter, himself once an out-standing athlete, is host to England's principal autumn Three-Day Event, and the atmosphere of his ancestral home and its surroundings adds im-measurably to the enjoyment both of competitors, and of spectators who come to watch fine horses and brave riders perform feats of skill and courage.

Burghley was the creation of William Cecil, first Lord Burghley, Queen Elizabeth I's great minister. The Cecils were a family of minor gentry from the Welsh borders, and William's grandfather, a supporter of Henry VII in his bid for the Crown, was the first to come to Stamford. William's father, who also supported the Tudor monarchy, bought the manor of Burghley in the 1520s. The estate grew in the following years as the lands belonging to the many local monasteries were dispersed.

Aerial view of Burghley in 1969, showing the house and part of the park. Features of Capability Brown's landscape which can clearly be seen are the Lake, the Lion Bridge which spans it and the Cutting which leads south from the Bridge.

Soon after his father's death in 1553, and with his mother still in residence, William Cecil started to remodel the manor house he had inherited, and building went on intermittently for more than thirty years, closely supervised by Cecil himself. He started with the east side in which are the double hammer-beamed Great Hall and the vast, vaulted Old Kitchen, now restored to what it was like in the nineteenth century with huge ovens and spits and innumerable brass cooking pots. The south side, which faces the lake and contains the main state rooms, was completed around 1564. Work was then interrupted, when Cecil turned his attention to his newly purchased estate at Theobalds, and then resumed in grander style some time after he was created Lord Burghley in 1571. He then built the west side, which is dated 1577. The north façade, the most imposing,

with an impressive projecting entrance porch, was the last to be finished
and bears the date 1587.

The house is constructed around an inner courtyard with an elaborate
clock tower as its centrepiece, and is built of the very hard local building
stone, the grey-gold Barnack rag. Each side is completely different, yet the
pronounced horizontal lines and the prominence of the windows give it an
appearance of overall unity of design.

William Cecil was one of the most remarkable men of the great
Elizabethan age. Trained as a lawyer, he served both Protector Somerset
and the Duke of Northumberland, regents in Edward VI's reign, but when
Mary restored Catholicism as the State religion, he resigned from his
office, and turned his attention to his country seat and started building.

Since 1550 he had looked after Elizabeth's estates, and on her accession
in 1558 she appointed him her First Secretary. For forty years, until his
death in 1598, he was her chief minister, becoming Lord Treasurer in
1572. It was a relationship of great mutual trust and respect—Elizabeth
said of him 'No prince in Europe hath such a counsellor as I have in mine.'
And although there were occasions when she grew impatient of her grave
adviser, throughout her reign and especially in the troubled early years she
relied heavily on his wisdom and experience.

Notoriously careful of the public purse, Cecil was extremely lavish with
his own, filled partly from the fruits of office. In addition to Burghley,
from 1564 he was building a new mansion for his second son, at Theobalds, near Cheshunt in Hertfordshire, which when finished was said to be
one of the greatest palaces ever built in England. At Theobalds he enter-
tained the Queen on twelve occasions. Cecil also built, for convenience,
a more modest house in London, on the north side of the Strand, near
where the Lyceum dance hall now stands—an area owned by the family

until the nineteenth century when it was sold to pay of extensive debts.

Cecil's buildings were on a vast scale partly because they were intended to entertain the Queen and her enormous entourage. But it was also an age of ostentation, and having himself made the transition from gentleman to nobleman, he wanted his family and their descendants to live in a style that fitted, and even enhanced, their status.

His second son Robert succeeded Cecil as adviser to the Queen, and later to James I. His eldest son Thomas, created Earl of Exeter on the same day in 1605 that his brother became Earl of Salisbury (a title turned down by the father on the grounds that it would involve him in too much expense), was in his early life a disappointment to him.

Both sons inherited their father's enthusiasm for building. In addition to a very fine house at Wimbledon, Thomas Cecil built Wothorpe, a mere mile away from Burghley, described as a 'dim reflection' of the big house, which he used, as Camden put it, 'to retire to out of the dust while Burghley was asweeping'. His brother remodelled both Beaufort House in London and Cranborne Manor in Dorset, and at the request of James I exchanged Theobalds, which James felt was altogether more suitable for a king than a subject, for the old royal palace at Hatfield. Robert Cecil then built the great house that stands there today, finishing it in 1611. From this point the Cecil family was divided into two great branches—the Salisbury line based on Cranborne and Hatfield and the Exeter line based on Burghley.

Burghley, not always a haven of peace, was a refuge for Royalist supporters in the Civil War, and in 1643 was besieged by Cromwell. He spent nearly three hours unsuccessfully bombarding the south front, but then carried the place after a further five hours of musket fighting. Traces of the battery can still be seen, but little damage was done and only six or seven

The south and west fronts from across the Lake.

Capability Brown's summer-house, in harmony with the intricate skyline of the house.

(Right) Brent geese on the south lawn, photographed during the World Championships in 1974. In the distance can be seen the Lamb Creep, a cross-country fence sited in one of the ancient avenues.

men were killed. None of the Exeter family was involved as the 4th Earl was only fifteen at the time.

The man under whom Burghley House probably achieved its greatest artistic glory was John Cecil, who became the 5th Earl of Exeter in 1678. He married the sister of the 1st Duke of Devonshire who about this time was rebuilding Chatsworth—scene today of one of England's oldest horse trials—in a style that fitted his new ducal status. Some of the finest craftsmen of the day worked at both houses, among them the French painter Laguerre, and his son-in-law, the master iron smith Tijou, who made the beautiful Golden Gate in the west front gatehouse at Burghley.

Around three sides of the courtyard the 5th Earl created the series of state rooms for which the house is famous, and which culminate in the incredibly lavish 'Heaven Room' on the south side. The room was painted by the Italian artist Verrio, who had been working on the state rooms at Windsor until James II abdicated and his Royal appointments were terminated. Throughout these rooms there are many fine Soho tapestries, and much exquisite carving, some by Grinling Gibbons and some by Thomas Maine and Jonathan Young.

On the ground floor, overlooking the lake, the 5th Earl also created the more intimate set of apartments which are still used by the family and in which Lord Exeter entertains the horse trials competitors and officials. In contrast to the slightly sombre, awe-inspiring atmosphere of the state rooms, this part of the house is light and comfortable. Now foxes' masks snarl at a pleasing combination of priceless works of art and personal favourites, among them a painting of the present Marquess of Exeter as Master of Foxhounds. But the rooms still owe much to the 5th Earl, with their stucco ceilings, moulded panelling and some especially good carving by Gibbons.

The 5th Earl travelled to the continent on at least four occasions and became an intimate friend of the Grand Duke of Tuscany who helped him to collect many of the great Italian master paintings. He died near Paris in 1700 at the age of fifty-three. The next great collector was the 9th Earl who succeeded fifty-four years later and added substantially to the Italian col-

12

lection. Burghley also contains outstanding works from other countries by such masters as Holbein, Breughel, Rembrandt, Van Dyck and Gainsborough. Indeed one of the great charms of Burghley is the amazing profusion of works of art of very high quality. In addition to the seven hundred or so paintings, the house is filled with fine furniture, and in the state rooms there are magnificent four-poster beds and marble fire-places with silver furnishings.

The 5th Earl left the family coffers severely depleted, and the state rooms, which were unfinished, were not used for more than fifty years. The 9th Earl when he succeeded in 1754 found Burghley greatly in need of renovation, and immediately consulted Capability Brown, the landscape architect, by that time already fairly well known. So began a twenty-five year association, one of the most important in Brown's career, which resulted in some dramatic changes in the surroundings, and—although Brown was not primarily an architect—some important alterations to the house.

Lancelot Brown, who came from Northumberland, must have been a very busy man: he had few contemporary rivals and the eighteenth-century fashion for creating natural landscape meant that his genius was much in demand. His landscaping seems to lend itself particularly well to cross-country courses, for there have been horse trials at Stowe, Wilton, Sherborne, Clandon Park, Chatsworth and Harewood, all of which owe something of their landscape to Brown. He is also thought to have modified some of William Kent's avenues at Badminton.

At Burghley the stables, a block of twenty-four stalls and eighteen loose boxes in a three-sided castellated courtyard; the orangery which is now the tea room; and the little summer house near the lake, were all designed by Brown. Brown was also responsible for raising the centre of the façade on the south front, where the second-storey windows are dummies, as the tall state rooms inside take up more than one floor in order to bring them to the level of the wings. He also pulled down a low wing on the west side of the north forecourt which matched the one that still exists, thus opening out what had been a courtyard enclosed on three sides.

But it was on the immediate surroundings of the house that Brown did his most dramatic work. Plans prepared for the 9th Earl in 1755 show that there were extensive formal gardens, with walks and terraces and such features as a bowling green, a pheasantry, a number of fish ponds, a wilderness and a vineyard, in a largely enclosed area of about thirty acres to the south and west of the house.

Brown wanted to create the impression that the house rose straight from the smooth green grass of its natural surroundings, so he swept away the formal gardens and levelled out the terraces. Water being an essential part of his schemes, he created the lake, using the small stream that later fed the trout hatcheries to flood a depression where there had previously been a large pond. He also designed the three-arched bridge, known as the Lion Bridge, that spans it. The ha-ha was built at the end of the century and fitted in with Brown's ideas, for it erased the visible barrier between the gardens and the park.

Brown also carried out extensive work on the park. Now covering fourteen hundred acres, and nearly seven miles in circumference, the park was originally much smaller. Fifty years after the house was completed, the southern boundary had been the wall that now divides the golf course from the rest of the park. This was the line of Ermine Street, the old Roman road from London to York, the fosse and vallum of which can still be easily identified in places. In the 1660s the 4th Earl had the ancient road diverted to its present course and considerably enlarged the park, enclosing it with the neat stone wall which is now the first sign of Burghley as you come up the Great North Road from the south. The park was again enlarged in the 1790s when the area along the Barnack Road was enclosed.

Many of the trees that grace the park today, mainly limes and oaks, were planted by the 5th Earl, or immediately after his time. Both the double-banked lime avenue at the end of the golf course, and Queen Anne's Avenue, also four rows of limes (the roads and tracks section of the horse trials follows one or the other) were planted by the early 1700s. The limes are now causing problems as they reach their maturity for they are susceptible to high winds, and every major gale brings casualties. In 1970, emergency action had to be taken on cross-country day when, as a result of the previous night's storm, Phase C was completely blocked by a fallen tree.

The plans of the park as it was before Brown made his alterations show many more trees than there are today, all standing to attention in straight lines. Brown planted some trees and moved others—he had invented a patent system for moving mature trees—using clumps and single trees to soften the straight lines of the avenues. Capability's Cutting, favourite site for a tricky obstacle, follows one of the old avenues to the arched South Gate, and was previously one of the drives to the house. The gradient was altered by Brown, possibly to make the drive less steep but also to fit in with his idea of providing a variety of views of the house on approach, since the Cutting itself obscures the view of the house.

Though William Cecil was more of an intellectual than a sportsman—there is a painting of him looking ill at ease astride a mule—there have been many connections between Burghley and sport since his time. The narrow light blue and white stripes of the Cecil colours were frequently seen at Stamford Races which from 1717 to 1873 were held on a racecourse just south of the park across the A1 near the airfield from where the RAF now

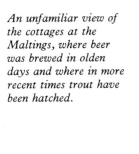

An unfamiliar view of the cottages at the Maltings, where beer was brewed in olden days and where in more recent times trout have been hatched.

fly their Harriers. The ruins of the grandstand can still be seen and the straight mile, said to have rivalled Newmarket and Doncaster in its excellence, can still be easily identified.

Brownlow, 2nd Marquess of Exeter (a marquessate was bestowed on the Exeter family in 1801), bred some very good horses at his Newmarket stud. From his famous mare Pocahontas (of whom no fewer than five hooves are preserved at Burghley) came many Classic winners. One of her sons, Stockwell, won both the St Leger and the Two Thousand Guineas, then himself sired many outstanding horses, including three successive winners of the St Leger in the 1860s.

The races were a great local occasion, with cock fighting—there was a cock pit at the George Hotel with room for four hundred spectators—and many other amusements. In 1809 Daniel Lambert, a hugely fat man from Leicester where he was the gaoler until his girth forced him to give up the job, came to exhibit himself but died suddenly before the races. At his peak he weighed 52 stones 11 pounds and it is after him that the enormous seat fence, Lambert's Sofa, is named.

With the death of the 2nd Marquess in 1867 Stamford Races lost their main supporter; the racecourse was soon closed and the straight mile was subjected to the steam plough.

There is good pheasant shooting at Burghley, and at different times the park has seen such games and sports as football, polo, hockey, cross-country running and drag hunting. The golf course—now invaded every year by the horse trials for the steeplechase course—was laid out by the present Marquess of Exeter's father, and the cricket ground by the 3rd Marquess who was a keen cricketer. The 3rd Marquess also built the trout hatcheries in which fish were raised until shortly before the horse trials were first held. There used to be many more pools than those used for the cross-country course, and the level of the water can be regulated. More recently trout have been hatched in the Maltings near by—used in the past for brewing beer—but they were never put in the lake where there is coarse fishing; some were sold, and some were released in Whitewater, near the racecourse.

Both the present Lord Exeter and his father hunted their own pack of foxhounds. The Burghley Hunt was started by Lord Exeter's father at the turn of the century as a pack of harriers, and the hunt servants always wore green livery. It lapsed during the First World War but was revived by Lord Exeter in the '30s and again in the '50s after another lapse during the Second World War. They hunted by invitation of the neighbouring packs, the Cottesmore and the Fitzwilliam, over their country; great sport was had, and nobody had to pay, although followers were expected to subscribe elsewhere. Both the hounds and the hunt horses were kept at Burghley. Sadly, when Lord Exeter gave up riding in 1967, the hunt was disbanded and the stables have since been empty.

Capability Brown's stables have never been used for the horse trials—except when Princess Anne's horse was stabled there in 1971—as in the early days they were occupied by the hunt horses. The permanent stables along the Barnack road near which the horse trials tented stables are erected were built towards the end of the last century, probably for the use of brood mares. There is a new horse trials office there now. The 'character' of the stables is Nimpy Holmes, a local recluse who lives all the year round in one of the loose boxes. He once saved Lord Exeter's horses from fire, and is a great reader—his bookshelf is above the manure heap—and he carries out many helpful tasks for the stable managers.

The present Lord Exeter will always be remembered in sporting history for the Gold Medal he won in the 400 m hurdles at the Olympic Games in Amsterdam in 1928; four years later he gained a Silver Medal for the 4 × 400 m relay at Los Angeles, and he has won dozens of other international titles. A true amateur, he managed on a minimum of training: in the later part of his career when he was an MP he would snatch an hour at the White City before the evening session at the House of Commons. But he always found it more difficult to prevent himself becoming stale than to get his body to peak fitness. The arthritis he now suffers in his hips is, he feels, more the product of hereditary shallow joints than the strain of athletics.

Forced to give up hunting, Lord Exeter still takes a close interest in sport, including the Three-Day Event, and he is the senior member of the International Olympic Committee. He has led a full and varied life. He was Member of Parliament for Peterborough from 1931 to 1943, was Governor of Bermuda for two years in the 40s, and has held many other official posts. He has also been closely involved in industry. Among other positions, he was Chairman of Birmid-Qualcast, a large engineering company; for many years a director of the National Provincial Bank; and later of the National Westminster after the amalgamation.

At Burghley he now farms about 4,000 acres, mainly arable apart from the park. Based on the Dairy Farm, another popular site for a difficult cross-country fence, he has one of the oldest Southdown flocks in the country. The care of his heritage at Burghley is one of his main concerns: the estate now belongs to a well-endowed charitable trust with the object of preserving it intact for future generations.

The towers and spires of the town of Stamford, one mile away across the River Welland in Lincolnshire, may have provided inspiration to William Cecil when he was designing Burghley. He must anyway have been deeply conscious of its beauty, for the top rooms have good views of Stamford, and from the centre room on the west side one sees the spires of All Saints and St Mary's, although some distance apart, in perfect alignment and on a misty day looking like one building. William Cecil chose to be buried in Stamford, in St Martin's, where there is an elaborate effigy of him, and where many of his descendants are also buried.

Lying at an ancient crossing of the River Welland, Stamford in medieval times was a great centre of religious learning, and had many religious houses, one of them in the vicinity of Burghley. And in the days when the Lincolnshire Wolds were covered with grazing sheep it was also an important wool market. It still has a remarkable number of fine buildings, mainly from the seventeenth and eighteenth centuries, and managed to escape the industrial expansion of the nineteenth century. In the 1840s the main railway to Scotland, which could easily have passed through Stamford, went instead to Peterborough.

A traditional stopping point on the old Great North Road, Stamford has many old inns but none has better connections with the horse trials than The George. Full of the flavour of coaching history and the days when it could accommodate eighty-six horses, The George is a largely early eighteenth century building but with its origins going back much further. It is here that the British team stays when Burghley is a team competition. The

horse trials organisation values highly the co-operativeness of the man-
agement, and the competitors appreciate the quality of the food.

Thus Burghley with its long history and connections provides a superb
setting for the Three-Day Event. It was envied even by Goering, Hitler's
right hand man, who according to a German pilot shot down in the war,
had given orders not to bomb the house, as he fancied it as his country seat
after the German invasion of England.

How fortunate the horse trials world is to have such a place for one of its
most important competitions.

*View through the main
gates towards the north
front, which is the most
ornate of the façades. It
was the last to be
completed and its date,
1587, can be seen above
the central doorway.*

17

CHAPTER 2

The Making of the Three-Day Event

JANE PONTIFEX

Harewood went out in a blaze of glory—almost literally. The summer of 1959 had been long, hot and bone-dry. The grass in Harewood Park was like spun glass, drained of colour, flat and slippery. Everywhere, notices warned about the danger of fire; sticks and brooms were stacked ready for use as beaters.

But the European Three-Day Event Championships there had been a triumph for Reg Hindley and his Yorkshire committee, climax of seven years' striving to establish Harewood as Britain's autumn Three-Day Event, complementary to Badminton in the spring and at last entrenched in Yorkshire under the patronage of the Princess Royal. Teams had entered in unprecedented numbers from all over Europe, the public had flocked to attend a great sporting occasion and it had been hailed as a resounding success.

Then it was all over. This was the end of the line: the estate's farming policy was changed and there was to be no more Harewood Three-Day Event.

It was a great blow to the British Horse Society. So much hard work, expertise and goodwill could not be lightly written off, and so a great drive was instigated to find a successor to Harewood. Lieutenant-Colonel Sandie Monro, the Combined Training Committee's Scottish member, travelled all over the north of England, investigating the possibilities of many a great estate at the suggestion of kindly-disposed landowners.

But a Three-Day Event needs more than so many acres of parkland on which to build a cross-country course, with a fine house as its focal point and a generous owner at its head. There must be a large expanse of flat—really flat—ground for the dressage arena and the still larger show jumping ring, big enough to surround with grandstands, and more space still for a township of tents and trade stands in suitable proximity.

There must be stabling, water, power and telephone cables, plenty of car parks, well-drained soil, several good approach roads, somewhere comfortable and convenient for a host of competitors and officials to stay—to say nothing of spectators—one or two biggish population centres within easy access and, above all, someone capable of a considerable feat of organisation, available for at least six months of the year and backed up by a number of horse-minded members of the local community, able to form a businesslike committee and to fill the myriad voluntary roles required in running a Three-Day Event.

1960 went by in fruitless search, but by 1961 the Marquess of Exeter had generously placed the park of his beautiful Elizabethan home, Burghley House, at the British Horse Society's disposal and Brigadier

James Grose, newly retired from the army and with more than a nodding acquaintance of horse trials, engaged to carry out the dual functions of Combined Training Field Officer to the BHS and Director of the brand-new Burghley Three-Day Event.

Lord Exeter, of course, was President of the organising committee, but he was no mere figurehead. Although he was a busy public figure, he always made a point of presiding over every committee meeting possible and took an intense interest in all the proceedings. He has imparted dynamic support and infectious enthusiasm to the entire undertaking, right from the start.

Vice-President was Sir Henry Tate, a truly active member and tireless worker, who believed in rolling his sleeves up and for whom nothing was too much trouble and no job too trivial in the good of the cause.

Mr John Langton, Burghley estate agent, Mr Giles Floyd, Lord Exeter's son-in-law and farms controller, and, of course, Mr Bill Thomson, BHS technical expert who was to be responsible for the course, made up the committee.

Bill Thomson took up residence that summer in his caravan, parked by the Maltings, and a lorry-load of stores arrived from Harewood—flags, posts, signs, tools, office equipment and eventually the office itself—a prefabricated wooden hut with a life expectancy of ten years, which had already done duty for seven and is still in use after seventeen more.

The hut was set up by the row of foaling boxes just inside the park wall and reached by a conveniently wide gateway off the Barnack road out of Stamford. There was a large Nissen hut to house the stores and a huge Dutch barn which was to serve as the grooms' canteen.

This little settlement was to become the nerve-centre of the Event. Mod. cons. were subsequently laid on and the hut later became the horse trials office. During the Event itself, the foaling boxes were supplemented by temporary stabling, caravans were imported for the grooms and a hard strip laid, on which the horses could be trotted up for the official inspection.

Officials at the first Event (right to left) *Brigadier James Grose, Sir Henry Tate, Lord Exeter, Mr J. C. P. Langton, Mr W. W. (Bill) Thomson and Mr Giles Floyd.*

1961. Brigadier Grose at his first competitors' briefing. Among those at the receiving end (right) were Anneli Drummond-Hay, Frank Weldon, Ben Jones, Patrick Conolly-Carew and Shelagh Kesler.

The Groses, meanwhile, moved into the White House in Stamford, which came to constitute unofficial headquarters during the winter months and home-from-home for many a visiting official.

If Burghley Three-Day Event was brand-new, at least the Combined Training set-up at the BHS office in Bedford Square in London, where I was secretary, was well established and Brigadier Grose lost no time in immersing himself in the minutiae of horse trials organisation. He was to be found at all the events that spring, notebook in hand, popping up in the most unlikely spots, questioning and assessing.

Once the spring horse trials were over, a room was hired in a private house in Stamford, a secondhand typewriter was purchased and Mrs Gladys Evans, wife of an RAF officer at Wittering (an establishment that has contributed enormously to the Three-Day Event, especially in the early years) installed as secretary. Sensible, efficient and lighthearted, she made the mould in which her successors were to be cast.

During his fifteen years as Director of Burghley, Brigadier Grose was to employ a number of girls as office staff and he always commanded their absolute loyalty. He was the boss, familiar with every detail of the organisation, but he knew just how much responsibility he could delegate and always got the best out of his staff—and in many cases their best was very good indeed. He had a well-developed sense of the ridiculous and was incapable of taking life too seriously; working for him at Burghley meant unstinting dedication to a job that was really well done, punctuated with outbursts of hilarity.

Stamford, and indeed the whole neighbourhood, felt itself to be charged with special responsibility for this important new Event and lost no time in rallying round. Local shops, printers, services and contractors were keen to get involved and the local Hunts (Burghley, Cottesmore, Fitzwilliam and Quorn), Army and Territorial Army units and, of course, the RAF, contributed the vital personnel without whom the top-heavy organisation of a Three-Day Event is powerless.

This strong local spirit has persisted. The programme contains a high proportion of local as well as national advertisements, and many local concerns contribute to the trade stand displays which are a particularly attractive feature of Burghley. Stamford sponsors one of the ancillary show jumping competitions and the Mayor of Stamford is an honoured guest at the event.

There were thirty-three entries for the horse trials in 1961. Twenty horses started and nine completed the final jumping test on the third day. But the first and much the biggest hurdle had been cleared: a new autumn Three-Day Event had been established, and it had run smoothly and well.

In 1962 Burghley really came into its own. Badminton, by now a by-word in Three-Day Event circles the world over, could not be moved from its early spring date, which ruled it out as a championship venue, yet Britain had been asked by the FEI once again to play host to the European Championships. Organisations with the capability and the facilities to run such championships were thin on the ground in those days and to refuse could have meant a serious setback to the sport as a whole.

This was to be the justification for all the long-term planning and the urgency in getting Burghley off the ground. The championships would be costly and the organisation a challenge, but Burghley was now a going concern and ought to be able to do it.

Through the good offices of Lord Gretton, who lived not far away, the Midlands brewery firm of Bass, Mitchell's and Butler undertook to sponsor the prize money and to present a new trophy, a welcome development at this juncture, as expenditure was to leap by almost fifty per cent.

Four nations took part. In addition to the home team there was Ireland, without whose competitors no British Three-Day Event would ever seem really complete; France, also a regular visitor; and the USSR, whose sole appearance in England had been at Harewood two years earlier, when the team had kept very much to themselves.

Not long before the competition, two huge horse boxes carrying the Russian horses lumbered into Stamford in the middle of the night, turned

1974. Jane Pontifex (on the right) and Mrs James Grose marking out the dressage arena.

Dressage test (Pauline Abell and Pilgrim II) in 1964, when seating was needed for only a small number of spectators.

into the darkened encampment off the Barnack road and unloaded by the light of headlights. The entire contingent had travelled all the way from Russia by road and sea in these boxes, taking more than a week on the journey.

The horses looked in pretty poor shape, but they picked up surprisingly well and went on to win the team championship. The Russians evidently enjoyed their visit to England and were finally waved away from Stamford on their return home, one of the riders sitting on the bonnet of a Land Rover and brandishing the smart new silver trophy.

Three peaceful years ensued, during which Burghley consolidated its position as an annual national event and also staged the Pony Club Horse Trials Championships. It was often difficult to make ends meet, but the organisation settled into its stride, improvements were gradually introduced and more and more people came to enjoy the pleasant, informal atmosphere at Burghley and to feel that a couple of late summer days engaged in watching horses competing in such lovely surroundings was time well spent.

Lord Exeter agreed to a modest levelling programme in the main arena, where the ground fell sharply away in one corner: he said that Capability Brown had laid out the grounds and he didn't want them changed by Incapability Anyone Else.

Familiarity is always reassuring and many faces became familiar at Burghley. Colonel Eve and Major Bevan were always in charge at the stables, to welcome competitors and to see that they had everything they needed. Brian Young was in charge of the collecting ring and the start and finish 'box' on cross-country day; John Stevens looked after the competitions held in the second arena and doubled with Bill Thomson as commentator on cross-country day; Charles Stratton stage-managed the main ring and all the show jumping.

Colonel Hickman was chief veterinary officer, Dr Parry recruited the local doctors and Mr George Gibson the vets. Mrs Atkinson drilled the Pony Club runners, mounted and on foot.

Woodhouse always contracted for the grandstands and temporary stabling, Claphams for the tents, and their respective foremen, Arthur White and Eric Billings, became part of the regular team, as did Mr Angell with his public address system and Mr Davey, who started laying telephone lines each year in the course of duty at RAF Wittering and continued to do so after he retired.

All these and many more—such as Mr Trowell (programme sellers), Mr Belton (scoreboard), Mr Wilcox (Burghley's clerk of works)—were familiar figures in key roles and, year by year, helped to give the Three-Day Event its friendly, efficient character. Some of them have since retired and others have joined their ranks, but a great many helpers have remained in their jobs ever since the first year.

Apart from general involvement as Combined Training Secretary, my own contribution in the early years was scoring and timekeeping. The first was already a familiar chore, the second a closely related activity which I had always wanted to bring under single control. At Burghley I had my chance to do so.

Timekeepers in those days for the speed and endurance test were supplied by pilots and navigators from RAF Wittering and it was my duty

Inspection during the World Championships, 1974. Michael Plumb of the USA shows Good Mixture to the Ground Jury. Colonel Eve, the stable manager, is on the right.

to brief them. Explaining the system—the independence of the phases, the recording of times and their transmission to the scorers—was all right, but my demonstration of working a chronometer left a good deal to be desired. The situation was saved by one of my listeners kindly taking the chronometer out of my hand, giving it a swift appraisal and passing it round to his fellows for inspection: for them such a simple mechanism was child's play.

From then on I had no further worries about timekeeping. Nor did I when, some years later, the RAF were obliged to withdraw and the British Cycling Federation was asked to provide the timekeepers. They were accustomed to posses of competitors flashing past in split seconds and to them one horse every four minutes posed no problems. And Mr Dowie and his friends brought their own chronometers.

Wittering also provided WRAF personnel as flag stewards for the check points on the roads and tracks phases, but these outposts in the countryside were considered unsuitable for girls on their own, so they were always deployed in pairs.

By 1966 the stage was set for another, even bigger, international event, the very first World Championships, with Burghley designated as its venue. It was acutely disappointing that an epidemic of swamp fever that year should bring a total ban on movement of horses in Europe. Ireland was outside the affected zone, however; the USSR and the USA flew their horses into the country direct; and Argentina sent a team across the Atlantic by sea.

The Argentinian horses arrived more than a month in advance in order to complete the required quarantine and this was arranged not far from Burghley, so that the riders could school and exercise their horses each day. Their determination was rewarded when their captain, Carlos Moratorio, won the championship on his Olympic silver medallist, Chalan.

To a visiting competitor, home is where the horse is, and the stables at Burghley are never a more homely spot than when there are teams from overseas: the only concession to protocol being the breaking of the appropriate national flag upon the arrival of each team. Otherwise, the village of horseboxes and caravans clustered round the stable manager's office, whiffs of cooking or snatches of music drifting over the air from the Dutch barn, is a peaceful, domestic scene. Set in a fold of the park, it seems far removed from the bustle and excitement of that other tented village just over the hill, laid out around the arena, where the competition itself is fought out.

The veterinary inspections at the stables, on the eve of the Event and again on the last morning, are friendly, informal affairs. But at those first World Championships, when the Russian stallion Paket was led out for the final inspection by his customary pair of attendants, one on either side, he was such a splendid sight, chestnut coat gleaming, neck arched, ears pricked, as he sprang up the gravel strip towards the judges, touching the ground in spots, that a burst of applause broke out from the onlookers— the only time I have ever known such a thing to happen.

For the next three years Burghley was a plain CCI (a mainly national event open to individual competitors invited from other countries), but even such comparatively peaceful years were not without drama. In 1964, for instance, Richard Meade on Barberry had won in such convincing style that the selection committee had had no alternative but to include him at

the last minute in the British team for the Olympic Games to be held that year in Tokyo.

'Double-take' at the stables.

Much the same thing happened in 1968, when Sheila Willcox, triple Badminton winner and a former European Champion, won at Burghley on Fair and Square. Again the selectors felt obliged to add her to the Olympic short list, but when she was asked to travel to Mexico as reserve rider, her own horse being omitted on the grounds of suspect soundness, she declined the invitation.

It was during this period that Burghley became firmly established as the national autumn Three-Day Event. Entries grew sufficiently to require two days for dressage and provide a full programme for spectators, with whom Burghley steadily grew in popularity.

The Three-Day Event's next international engagement was in 1971, when Burghley was designated the European Championships. By now the formula had been adopted whereby the winning nation played host to the next championship, and Britain had won the European Championships at Haras-du-Pin, in France, in 1969. This was the year in which Raleigh, another 'local' firm, based as they were at Nottingham, took over the sponsorship of Burghley horse trials.

The inclusion of Princess Anne in the British team and the presence of the Queen added greatly to the excitement. They also added a fresh dimension, incidentally, to my own job.

By then I had left the BHS, handing over the scoring to my successor, Eileen Thomas, and acted instead as press officer. To the usual job of providing facilities and information for the press and generally helping them as much as possible was added the new and often conflicting duty of preventing the press from interfering with the Royal team member's performance by singling her out for their special attention.

The 'equestrian' press were no problem, but the 'news' press, who turned up in strength but knew nothing about a Three-Day Event or the

(Left) *The other side of the picture: press photographers snapped by Jane Pontifex.*

(Right) *Capacity crowd. A sea of faces forms the backcloth for Richard Meade and Wayfarer on their way to a clear round during the World Championships in 1974.*

stresses it imposed on competitors, needed a lot of help as well as occasional restraining.

A few over-enthusiastic newshounds have given their colleagues a bad reputation which is quite undeserved. The press are people with a job to do—which is also going to benefit the Event in publicity—the job of getting a picture or a story of one who, after all, cannot help being 'news', and they are understandably indignant if they are prevented from doing that job. They are a cheerful, friendly breed, very appreciative of any help one can give them and, in my experience, if they are given a fair deal they never fail to give a fair deal in return.

On these occasions, whichever of Princess Anne's private detectives is on duty is always a tower of strength. They are very nice, tactful, reasonable, men, liked and respected by the press, and they handle this aspect of their job extremely well.

Being press officer enables one to get out on the course and see something of the competition—a revelation to me, after years of being bottled up in a tent as scorer. Once, when I was driving a Range Rover full of press photographers, some clinging to the tailboard, as fast as I dared across the open park in an attempt to reach the finish before Princess Anne completed a brilliant round on Doublet, a cry went up behind me, 'Stop! You've dropped Roger!' Horrified at what I had done, I backed up to where Roger was picking himself up off the grass, but he was quite unconcerned and only worried about his camera, which luckily was also unscathed.

Standing back, waiting for my charges to take their pictures at a fence before moving on, I have seen some amusing sights: a very old lady sitting patiently on a deck-stool alone in the middle of the park; dogs tied up to guard coats and picnic hampers while their owners surged forward to watch a horse negotiate the Trout Hatchery; a tiny baby fast asleep in a shopping basket under a tree.

Once I found a lady's handbag left on the ground, so I picked it up and took it to the police caravan. I then fell in with some friends, one of whom was bewailing the loss of her handbag, convinced that she would never see it or its contents again, while her companion assured her that, at *Burghley*, she was sure to get it safely back. Their surprise on recognizing my description of the bag I had just handed in may be imagined, as may be the owner's delight on reclaiming it intact a few moments later.

In 1974 Burghley staged the World Championships once more, Britain having won the team title at Punchestown four years previously. This time there were no restrictions and ten nations entered teams. It was a tremendous challenge to the organisation.

An international championship poses all sorts of extra problems. Visiting teams—riders and officials—are put up at the host nation's expense, but they bring with them a train of wives, parents and other supporters who, naturally enough, want to stay in the same hotel, though this must be at their own expense.

Good hotel accommodation in Stamford is very limited and rooms must also be booked further afield, but no team must be allowed to feel it has come off worse than the others, and if two teams are booked in to the same hotel, it should be ensured that they are from friendly nations who are likely to get on well together. The same considerations apply in the allocation of stabling and of grooms' caravans.

Transport must be provided, and vehicles for the use of each team are generally loaned by local motor dealers.

A liaison officer is appointed for each team, but this is a difficult and demanding job and suitable candidates are scarce. Not only must they be able to speak the language fluently, they must have a thorough knowledge of the technicalities of a Three-Day Event and be able to explain regulations and instructions; they must familiarize themselves with the organisation, so that they know exactly how and where to find the answers to any questions that may be fired at them; they must accompany their team to all functions, official and social; and they must identify themselves with their team's interests and win the trust of its members.

Masters of Eventing. The Marquess of Exeter with the Duke of Beaufort at the first Burghley Horse Trials in 1961.

(Right) Miss Edna Stokes, who has worked in the Trials office since 1963.

27

A good liaison officer is invaluable to both team and organiser and Burghley has always been lucky in finding superb people—most of them girls—to do the job.

A certain amount of entertainment is laid on for the visitors, and local families have always been most generous in inviting teams to their homes and making up parties for the ball which the Cottesmore Hunt generally runs in conjunction with the horse trials. On the first evening of the Event a cocktail party is held at Burghley House, when Lord and Lady Exeter welcome all the competitors and officials. This makes a great start to the four days during which all those involved in the Event are going to be thrown so closely together.

Like many others, I suppose, the Three-Day Event world is a fairly tight little circle and friendships are struck up and renewed in the different countries where international events are held. Competitors often crop up again and again, then perhaps return as team officials and eventually even as judges and technical delegates.

Early in 1974 Brigadier Grose suffered a heart attack. He made a good recovery and his organisation of the World Championships was better than ever, but it made him face up to the decision to retire. He continued for one more year and then bowed out in 1976.

The new Director was Major Andrew Burnaby-Atkins and the smoothness with which the organisational machine continued to function would have surprised Brigadier Grose himself. Its efficiency gave the new Director a chance to find his feet before tackling his first official international event, the European Championships of 1977.

One of the assets Major Burnaby-Atkins had inherited was Edna Stokes, senior member of the office staff for fifteen years, and he now persuaded Jill Neill, who had earlier worked for seven years with Brigadier Grose, to rejoin her. Their incalculable contribution and the hard work of the loyal volunteers who had played their part since the Event's inception produced a magnificent show, which gave a further boost to the Event's attendance and turnover—by now increased tenfold since the first year.

Britain regained the team title and Lucinda Prior-Palmer made history by becoming European Champion for the second time in succession.

But I only learned about it all secondhand because, on arrival in Stamford for the great occasion, a disc in my back folded up and with it my seventeen-year record at Burghley. I spent that week (and the next three) flat on my back in Stamford Hospital, watching as much of the Event as I could see on my borrowed TV set, with nurses popping in to snatch a quick look at every possible opportunity, and being regaled by graphic accounts of the day's happenings each evening from the kind friends who came to visit me.

One of the visitors was Major Burnaby-Atkins, who looked drawn and tired, despite his elation at the success of the Event. By the end of the year he had decided to resign on account of ill-health and Charles Stratton, closely associated with Burghley ever since it started, was appointed to succeed him as Director.

In 1978 Burghley is to stage the European Junior Championships in conjunction with the annual Three-Day Event and no doubt the senior championships will be back before long. Long may Burghley continue to build on its unsurpassed reputation for superb presentation of such landmarks in equestrian history!

On Course

One of the most important people in the staging of Burghley is Bill Thomson, who designs and builds the cross-country courses, thus setting the scene in which the drama of the second day unfolds. He has been responsible for the course since Burghley was first held in 1961, with only one year off, in 1975. Before that he worked at Harewood, Burghley's forerunner as the Northern Three-Day Event. Trained as a veterinary surgeon, he gave up the profession to become a full-time course-builder in the 1950s. Now, as the British Horse Society's senior course-builder, he designs and advises on many other courses, and his duties keep him so busy that in recent years he has rarely had a chance to go abroad to study other championship courses.

Course-building is a subtle art and requires not only a deep knowledge of the way horses jump and how they think, but also a peculiar type of imagination. Bill Thomson, a quiet, sensitive man, is an expert. At Burghley he has dreamed up an astonishing number of new fences, using to the full the limited number of natural features. He has, for instance, devised many different problems in the ditch below the arena area—a footbridge, a treakehner, and now the double coffin, are among the most ingenious. At the mound on the Waterloo Plain, a site which has been used thirteen times, there have been a wide variety of different drop fences. He has also built some permanent fences, such as the Leaf Pit and the Sunken Wall, which remain more or less unchanged although they are not always included.

The course is given a fresh look every year with a number of new fences —there are always more for an international team championship and the necessity of constantly producing new ideas worries Thomson. He has moments of despair when the inspiration seems to dry up, but experience has made him more confident that the course will turn out well in the end, and he finds that once he has thought up two or three new ideas the rest usually fall into place. Burghley occupies his mind throughout the year; he lives conveniently near Stamford and works at Burghley intermittently. In a normal year he starts construction work in June but if there are many new fences to be built, as in 1978 when he devised a second course for the Junior European Championships, he starts soon after the New Year.

In 1961, his first year, he spent two weeks plodding round the park to familiarise himself with the features. Now, seventeen years later, he knows every mound and indentation so well that he can design fences from his armchair. He works out his ideas with rough sketches, and before carrying out any construction work he pegs out the fence on the site, using string to represent the rails.

In the early days, money was scarce, but now Thomson is given more or less a free hand. In 1962 the cost of the course and the maintenance of the ground throughout the year was about £2,000; in 1977 the course alone cost £10,000. The increase is due partly to constantly rising prices, but also to the increase in the size and quality of the timber, a great deal of which is needed to build the big, solid fences now demanded. For example, in 1977 the construction of all the new fences used about 250 trees: fifteen were needed for the Waterloo Rails alone. Thomson goes to great lengths to avoid the possibility of fences being broken during the competition. No timber that is remotely breakable is left for more than two years and when he builds a new fence, even if it is replacing an old one, he uses nearly all new timber as the posts may be rotten at their base.

In the '60s, rails and posts could easily be handled by two men; now they have to be put into position by tractor—thus greatly increasing the cost. Similarly, in the past most of the fence building was done by Thomson with the help of one estate worker but now a firm of general contractors is employed. The estate is not able to provide enough suitable timber so it is brought in from outside—though the estate sawmill carries out all the cutting. Men from the estate also put up the chestnut paling and the string for controlling the crowd.

The fences at Burghley are beautifully finished, with Christmas trees used liberally, both for filling in and for decoration. The fence flags have done long service, having been in use since 1959, when they were made for the European Championships at Harewood.

The scope for changing the track of the cross-country course is limited. With a course of four miles or more the park does not provide much extra room and the car parks make increasing encroachments. The lake breaks up the available ground and there has been only one way round it—through Chabonel Spinney. The idea of jumping over the narrow channel by the bridge was suggested but turned down by Lord Exeter. Although the

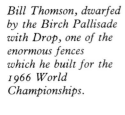

Bill Thomson, dwarfed by the Birch Pallisade with Drop, one of the enormous fences which he built for the 1966 World Championships.

(Above) *The Spray Fence, one of Bill Thomson's most ingenious creations, also built for the World Championships in 1966. Water was pumped from the lake to maintain the spray.* (Below) *Post and rails fence on the steeplechase course (which in 1964/5 was sited between the Dairy Farm and the Lake), here negotiated by Martin Whiteley and The Poacher.*

course does sometimes breach the park walls—over the sunken wall in the area of the Bull Pens—it never goes far in this direction. It is more convenient for spectators if it is kept within a fairly compact area.

Bill Thomson is also responsible for the other phases of the speed and endurance section, and it was largely due to him that the FEI decided to drop Phase E from Three-Day Events. This phase, also known as the 'run-in', was about half a mile long and followed the cross-country. It had to be ridden at a slow canter. It greatly complicated the problem of siting the start and finish box—so it was a relief to Thomson when it was dropped in 1967. The roads and tracks—Phases A and C—are particularly attractive at Burghley, as much of the route follows the ancient avenues. Since the going is good and as there are no steep hills this section is not unduly taxing for the horses.

The steeplechase course has now found a permanent home on the golf course, where the closely mown grass of the fairways provides excellent and very fast going. For the first three years it was sited in the deer park beyond the golf course, in the area (now plough) between the great double avenues of limes: the southernmost part of the park bordering the A1. In 1964/5 a tortuous course was laid out for the steeplechase between the Dairy Farm and the Lake. This was convenient for spectators but posed problems for horses and riders, so for the 1966 World Championships it was moved to the golf course where it has been sited ever since.

Thomson believes that the best horses will always win and that it is not necessary for the course to cause too much grief. A few years ago it was considered normal for only about 30 per cent of competitors to complete the cross-country, but Thomson has always felt that this is unacceptable, and has designed his courses at Burghley accordingly. In percentage terms most trouble was caused by the course of 1968 when only 41 per cent of the starters finished the competition; in 1966, 54 per cent finished; in 1971, 68 per cent. Recently the courses have been easier in relation to the standard of the competitors for in 1976, 70 per cent of the starters completed the cross-country and in 1977, 80 per cent—the highest number ever.

Thomson has a finely tuned sense of what is possible in terms of problem fences, and his obstacles have never placed unreasonable demands on the horses. He believes that straightforward fences, such as parallels or tables, on level ground present no difficulties even at maximum dimensions. The real skill in course-building lies in correctly gauging the problem fences. But while there have been few falls at the big spreads at Burghley, there have been many uncomfortable jumps. Lucinda Prior-Palmer in the account of her round in 1977 relates how George gave her a nervous moment when he stood off a stride too far at the Troughs. Such fences certainly instil respect in the riders, and the Americans were undoubtedly very impressed by the sheer size of the course in 1974.

Another consideration in the mind of the course-builder is that he should provide entertainment for the spectators. Interesting fences are often grouped closely together and various devices are used for making the jumps more spectacular—digging the ditches deep, making the birch of an open ditch start from the bottom of the ditch, and digging the uprights for a trakehner into the bottom of the ditch. These features generally make more impression on the crowd and possibly on the rider than on the average horse. Drops are always dramatic: some are simple to jump, such as the Leaf Pit, while others like those at the Waterloo Plain and the rails off

the Dairy Farm Mound require a bold horse and attacking approach.

Many famous riders have fallen in the Trout Hatcheries—much to the delight of spectators—generally because they have either hit the fence at the brink, or taken it too fast. The suggestion that there is a hole in the bottom angers Thomson, for he takes immense trouble to ensure that the base is firm. In the first year there *was* a hole, created without Thomson's knowledge by a tractor which spun a wheel while attempting to put the log in place. Now both hatcheries have firm rubble bases.

The course always includes fences which offer a choice of approach and the possibility of gaining time by jumping a more difficult route. For a team competition these alternatives have to be very delicately balanced, as a rider under orders is less likely to take risks for the sake of saving a few time penalties. In the 1974 World Championships, Bridget Parker riding Cornish Gold, the first of the British Team to go, ran out attempting the shorter route over the corner of the Bull Pens. The word went round, and no-one else considered it worth the risk.

In a normal year the course must offer the good individual a substantial advantage over the mediocre one. The shorter route can be much more difficult if it offers a worthwhile time-saving.

When he is designing the course for a CCIO, Bill Thomson has to take other factors into consideration. In the past, championship courses have always been bigger and more challenging than the others. The maximum permitted spread for a fence is 6 ft. 6 in., as opposed to 6ft. 2 in. for standard competitions. The courses are also considerably longer.

As some of the teams come from countries where Eventing is a very narrow-based sport there is a wide variation in the standard of the competitors. Thus the problem for the course-builder lies in devising a course

First view of Capability's Cutting, now a familiar feature of the Burghley course. Frank Weldon (centre) watches John Tulloch pace out his proposed route. Among those watching are Lord Exeter and Bill Thomson.

33

Burghley's best-known obstacles: the Trout Hatcheries. (Above) First to test the water in 1961 was Badminton's future course-builder. (Below) Eleven years later, Anna Collins riding Think Lucky was one of five competitors to sample its flavour.

that is sufficiently difficult to provide a satisfactory test for the best teams while not resulting in the wholesale elimination of the worst.

The severity of a championship course depends primarily on the quality of the competitors expected to take part, and it is preferable that enough teams should be left in the competition to make the show jumping interesting for spectators on the final day. Taking part in the 1977 European Championships there were seven teams, some of them of only average ability, so the cross-country course was not especially difficult; whereas in the 1974 World Championships, when there were ten teams and a higher standard of entry, Bill Thomson was able to make the course more demanding.

In the past, the wide divergence in the standard of competitors for team competitions applied also to the individual competitions (CCIs). Qualifications were minimal—which meant that the courses had to cater not only for the top horses and riders but also for inexperienced ones, who in some cases were entering for their first Three-Day Event. The courses then were smaller than they are now, as the maximum height for the fences was 3 ft. 9. Since 1972, when the individual competition became a championship Three-Day Event, the maximum height of the fences has been 3 ft. 11 —the same as for a CCIO. And in 1975 the qualifications were considerably tightened up so that nowadays they preclude inexperienced horses and riders from taking part at Burghley.

There have nearly always been foreign entries for the CCIs at Burghley, but in recent years the leading English horses have been absent. The international team championships, when held abroad, have usually been within a few weeks of Burghley—so our team horses have not been entered, though the team riders have often competed on other horses.

Bill Thomson does not have the final say on his courses at Burghley, as they have to be passed by an inspection panel, consisting of three senior officials appointed by the British Horse Society. It is usually only a matter of deciding the final height of the fences, but the panel has the authority to make more substantial alterations if it considers it necessary. The panel also inspects the course for a CCIO, but it carries no official power to approve it, and the technical delegate has the final responsibility for checking the fences.

On cross-country day, Bill Thomson is never able to be on the course watching the action. He sees it on closed-circuit television in Control (an army truck), where he provides the commentary for the public address system. In Control the progress of each horse is plotted on a model which is kept up to date minute-by-minute with the help of radio reports from each fence and from other strategic points. If the course becomes blocked the decision has to be made to stop the next horses—and with up to twenty competitors on the course at one time (including roads and tracks and steeplechase), the decision has far-reaching effects. For Thomson, it is a nerve-wracking occasion, as much of the responsibility for the afternoon's events lies with him. In spite of his breadth of experience there is always the possibility that he has made a miscalculation and that the course-builder's nightmare, a 'bogey' fence, will develop. In practice, it never has, but he has a traumatic time waiting for the first few horses to prove the course is jumpable. This is the moment of truth when all the planning and work of the past months are put to the test.

CHAPTER 4 # A Place of Learning

CHRIS COLLINS

For the competitor, Eventing is a voyage of discovery, new complexities being constantly unfolded along the way. Mine has been far from a success story, but it may be that something can be gleaned from my experiences. Although I have ridden in lots of Three-Day Events, my six rides at Burghley mirror the various ups and downs I have been through.

I first rode there in 1970 on Tawny Port. He was a fine schoolmaster. Correctly ridden at his own pace he would jump almost anything but would normally punish any attempt to hustle him by falling or refusing. Most of the 620 cross-country penalties we incurred in our two-year association arose from my failure to come to terms with this.

I arrived at Burghley determined to finish substantially higher than my third from last place at Badminton that spring. I was budgeting for a bad dressage but this was to be shrugged off with maximum bonus on the steeplechase and a good cross-country.

The dressage went as expected. In those days it was a struggle for me to keep my feet in the stirrups let alone have a horse on the bit performing complicated movements.

I came up to the start of the steeple in a very positive frame of mind and we set off at a fast gallop. The pace was too much for Tawny and he dived long and low through most of the fences. Long before the finish he was a tired horse. At lthe last, which in those days was an open ditch, I asked him for a final big effort. He ignored my offices, crashed through it and fell.

The long Phase C of a Three-Day Event affords ample time for repentance over steeplechase errors. By the end of it I had decided not to do the cross-country, being already effectively out of the competition with the 60 penalties, and to save him for another day.

My first appearance at Burghley had ended prematurely in total defeat. In the following year—1971—the European Championships were held, and as I was still far from being in this league, the opportunity to avenge my inauspicious début did not present itself until 1972. I had by now sold Tawny Port and this year was riding Flint Hill whose preparation had gone quite well.

He was pretty explosive in the dressage but his mark was somewhere in the middle of the field. Thanks to an unpleasant fortnight in Germany that summer under a top dressage Gruppenführer, I was by now beginning to move up from the bottom of this particular department. In the steeplechase I managed to achieve no penalties without taking risks. The time was easily achieved, but I was still pleased to be setting off around the cross-country intact and in touch.

He went away like a lion, but a lot of fight went out of him landing down the Leaf Pit, only Fence 4, and then infuriatingly stopped a fence or two later at the Coffin. He jumped it the second time but from then on was a dying horse. He finally ground to a halt twice when required to jump up a couple of banks out by the Bull Pens. Not having the heart to present him a third time, I retired. It took a long time to walk back from the far end of the park. It transpired afterwards that his back was wrong and I think he probably tweaked it landing down the drop of the Leaf Pit.

Again there was a defeat to be shrugged off. At 5.30 am the next day I left Leicestershire for the North to ride a gallop on Hilbirio who Arthur Stephenson was preparing for the Norwegian Grand National. The raw contact with racehorses in the early morning and the prospect of the big race ahead soon obliterated the previous day.

In the following year—1973—there were no grounds for optimism. My spring Eventing had been washed away by the cough and I myself had received something of a battering, having since January broken my arm, some bones in my feet and a collar bone in various racing and hunting falls. Furthermore, Centurian had stopped and fallen at both Annick and Osberton. Being the Marshal Ney of Event Horses he had only made these mistakes because there was something wrong with his back. He therefore had to spend the time between Osberton and Burghley with Mr Ashby who daily worked over him with his machines. He was also walking and trotting on the hills for three hours each day. He had very little fast work and even less dressage. At a good work-out on the old Richmond gallops a week before it was clear that his fitness was not good.

However, whatever one's prospects it is always a pleasure to arrive at Burghley. The friendly atmosphere is set in the stables, where nothing is too much trouble for Colonel Stephen Eve and Major Geoffrey Bevan, pillars respectively of the Cottesmore and Quorn, where Geoffrey, though rising eighty, still cuts a tremendous dash in his black cutaway and chocolate breeches. In international years Geoffrey is shamelessly partisan, loudly referring to those of different ideology and former war opponents by various colloquialisms for their local dishes, etc.

The day before the dressage I had had a rough day in Holland. I had been over to discuss the possible sale of my business to a large international group. Just as some people when buying a horse point out its faults, so they had run down our operation in an attempt to lower the price. For the early part of the day my mind kept returning to this and I eventually decided to call off the deal. To clear my mind I rang the Finance Director from the wooden stable office and asked him to let the Dutch know. Only then was I able to give full concentration to the important business of settling Centurian.

As sometimes happens, from an almost hopeless preparation, things went well. Centurian did the best test of his life and was generously marked. At the end of the dressage he was, to the astonishment of many people, lying in 4th place.

The next day I was determined not to sacrifice my good dressage score with a silly mistake and, in view of Centurian's doubtful fitness, planned to err on the slow side. The final straight of the steeplechase was very hard and I did not like to ride him out on it so incurred 8 time penalties. A steady clear on the cross-country left us at the end of the day in 6th place. A clear round the following day put us back up to 4th. I was thrilled with Centurian. He had displayed total honesty in the cross-country and been a

Chris Collins and the game of snakes and ladders. (Left) 1970: downward spiral as Tawny Port crashes through the last steeplechase fence. (Right, above) 1973: up the ladder, with Centurian on his way to a clear in the cross-country. (Right, below) 1974: on his way down again, as Smokey attempts to bank the Log Pile.

model of decorum in the other two phases.

After it was all over I managed to buy Smokey from William Powell-Harris. I had long admired this great horse from afar. In the dressage he never deigned to do more than 'sketch the movements required', as one commentator put it, and usually knocked down two or three show jumps, but in the cross-country he was supreme. I drove home down the A1, sure that the tide of my Eventing had at last turned.

By the World Championships in 1974 I had progressed to being in the team with Smokey. I arrived at Burghley convinced that he was the greatest cross-country horse in the world. I hoped that the course would be difficult enough and that I would be allowed to go fast.

He went reasonably well in the dressage for a 61 and the score held up better than expected over the second day, the leaders being in the mid 40s. Early on the evening before the cross-country we were summoned to our Chef d'Equipe Colonel Bill Lithgow's bedroom in The George, where he was painfully propped up in a chair suffering from five ribs broken in Tuesday evening's donkey racing. Making no concession to his injuries, Colonel Bill gave us a detailed and thorough briefing. On speed he was quite clear. 'We'll win by going fast. If any of you come back without maximum bonus and without an exhausted horse I'll want to know the reason why.' I was cleared for a real cut.

Cross-country day was airless and sultry. On the $2\frac{1}{2}$ mile steeplechase I was too fast. Despite easing up from the last fence I was still 12 to 15 seconds under. With the extra half mile this was a bad mistake. Smokey was blown and none too sound for the first kilometre of Phase C. It was a long hike and the heavy atmosphere in the woods did not aid recovery. However, he was himself again by the time we were back in the box.

Already Hugh Thomas had done a good fast round on Playamar. At that point no part of the course was causing particular difficulties, so I set off like the clappers. Smokey hit the big parallel at 4 but jumped the Double Coffin very neatly, made nothing of the next two and then ran on to Fence 7, a narrow log bank with rail beyond, at a good hand gallop. Rather than kick on for a stand-back I sat up for a waiting stride. It was a simple fence for him to pop. The Irish in him came out and he tried to bank what wasn't there. Inevitably we were turned over by the far rail. In one sickening moment our chance had gone. He was up and I was on pretty quickly. It was a team competition, a good time was important so I kicked on.

The course went on and on and Smokey dealt with fence after fence perfectly, but was getting tired. Finally at the Waterloo Rails he hit the top hard and landed vertically down the drop. Another 60 penalties and this time I was a bit dazed. Normally I would not have gone on but it was necessary to finish. Smokey was whacked. He splashed through the open water, heaved himself up the next bank, trotted through the Trout Hatchery, then completed the rest of the course on courage.

In a team, failure is very public. There can be no shrugging of shoulders and turning to the next item on the agenda. Rather one slinks around like a whipped dog, apologising to everyone in sight. Smokey was distressed after the cross-country and had to be given a few shots to get him back for the next day. He showed that there was no damage by jumping a clear round.

As is history, the Americans demonstrated their class with a convincing win and poor Mark Phillips had to withdraw Columbus with an injured hock having run into a clear lead after the cross-country.

As I drove down the A1 I reflected that Eventing was like Snakes and Ladders. After years of effort I had painstakingly climbed up a few ladders. Now with this reversal I had slithered down a really long snake. Over the months that followed I analysed and re-analysed what went wrong. In the end I put it down to several things: having an insufficiently surgical attitude, going too fast, not getting his fitness right, the hot weather—most of which were my fault and which I would try to avoid in the future.

I missed the 1975 Burghley, as the ground was too hard for Centurian and Smokey had a suspicion of leg trouble. In fact that autumn had been touch and go for me for a while as I had had a struggle to get back from crushing some vertebrae in a racing fall at Cheltenham.

For the 1976 Burghley I had Radway, a young horse of great promise. My mood was one of cautious optimism and of great interest to see how he would perform. The previous year he had gone extremely well at Boekelo over a difficult course, but because of fog there had been an interval between the second roads and tracks and the cross-country, which prevented it being a proper test of stamina. He had also won his three One-Day Events that autumn but it was possible that he was something of a chestnut 'Flash Harry' and an unknown quantity when the chips were really down.

After the dressage we were only just in touch with 72, but as it turned out the competition was to hinge on the steeplechase phase. Because of the hard ground this had been moved from the golf course to a stubble field. But then it had done nothing but rain. In consequence the going was very heavy and some of the early horses I saw could barely raise a canter at the finish. It was obviously vital to get the pace right. Not to go too slowly and get unnecessary penalties but not to go too fast and burst the horse either.

Radway set off like a dervish and I kept a real good hold of him. Round the first and second circuits he was virtually on time and still strong. Half way round the third circuit he 'went' quickly and finished a very tired

Top of the ladder. Chris and Smokey clear the Double Coffin during the European Championships in 1977, when with the fastest round of the day they helped the British Team to a memorable victory.

horse, but in a good time.

He recovered by the end of Phase C but was not too full of himself. He did not take hold when we set off on the cross-country, so remembering Smokey I let him go his own pace. He was jumping rather too high in the air without going properly forward and made one or two awkward leaps. We then met the Coffin on a stride to stand off and at the last minute he stopped—an infuriating error on my part as he would have jumped it with maximum pressure. He made nothing of it the second time and I gave him a real shaking-up for the Trout Hatchery.

As we were now effectively out of the competition I did not hurry him, and concentrated on giving him a good school. The further he went the better he went and he came back a more mature horse. I was displeased with the present but pleased for the future. He had taken another stepping-stone in his career and could now go to Badminton the following spring.

1977 was again an international year and by now Smokey and I had climbed back up enough ladders to be in the Team again. I was conscious that a repeat of my 1974 performance would brand me for ever as unreliable, yet I felt it would be a pity to go too steadily on Smokey. He was a proven fast horse and furthermore rather difficult to ride slowly.

I was keen to go early so that we could do our dressage before a crowd built up. I had by now worked out an elaborate pre-dressage rigmarole to settle Smokey. During the week in which we were there before the Event I had boxed him over to Leicestershire and taken him out on the roads for soothing hacks away from the competition atmosphere. On the morning of his test he went off to a nearby indoor school for a thirty-minute loose canter then came by box to the nearest possible point to the dressage so as not to be distracted by any cross-country fences. A jump to Smokey is like a red rag to a bull, he so loves the cross-country. My elaborate manoeuvres caused some merriment, but nevertheless except for jogging in the walk he did a good test.

I discussed tactics with our new Chef, Tadzik Kopanski. I suggested that going first I must try to go not too fast but not unnecessarily slowly. The course was not difficult but long enough to be a test of stamina and judgement of pace. Tadzik smiled and ordered me to 'get it right'.

Smokey did a perfect steeple. Standing far back but safely at most of the fences, he finished on the bit eight seconds under. He was blowing more than I expected. I had thought the time would be easy as the course was in excellent fast shape. In fact for some mysterious reason it was to cause quite a bit of trouble.

We slogged on round Phase C and eventually got back to the box. I

was seventh to go and the first of the British so there was not much that Tadzik and Richard Meade could tell me; the performances of the six continentals in front not being regarded as a certain guide.

We were soon being counted down and I let Smokey set off at his own pace. Unlike his fiery attack of a One-Day Event course, he did not really take hold of the bit. Over the first two as if they were hurdles, then as late as possible a steady before popping neatly down the Leaf Pit. Over the spread of hedges at an angle with a bit of an attack. A run into the hand before riding on at the Witch Way combination. So it went on with Smokey making little of the fences. Not travelling particularly fast but possibly taking more of a hold as time went on. A great leap at the Diamonds, easily over the Hayracks and a long run down to the gates. Now, with the edge off him, a need to set him up a little in front of the big parallels. Still the course went on and on. We were getting round it with a minimum of fuss and a certain precision but because of its great length and Smokey tiring all the while, with no great exhilaration.

Into the last mile, and it was necessary to cheer him on with a bit of pressure at some of the big fences. Here a shake-up, there a slap with the whip. A particularly tired leap at the third last. 'Come on, Smokey' I shouted and kicked him up into the bridle. Well over the second last. Over the last and on to the line. He pulled up blowing and whacked. As we walked back to the box Tadzik galloped up. I told him it was OK and anxiously asked about the time, half fearing I had not gone particularly fast. Tadzik rechecked his watch: 'According to me 15 seconds under!'

At the end of the day the British Team was in the lead and I was in 4th place, with the fastest time. Alas, in the show jumping we had two down and dropped to 7th. However, Lucinda moved up to win and the Team also won which was the main thing. I had personally come near to a satisfactory performance only to slither down a small snake on the last day. Back to the drawing board again!

As we lined up for the prize giving I felt disappointed over the jumping, proud to be involved in a British victory, and enormously privileged to ride Smokey. Getting off him for the last time in the collecting ring afterwards I was a little sad to think that we would not be working together again until after Christmas.

So ended my latest Burghley. In retrospect my mistakes look glaringly obvious. It took me a long time to realize that the old racing adage of 'kick on regardless' was a penalty-producer of the first order. The hard lesson of falls and refusals is that safety and precision are as important as speed in the delivery of a fast clear round.

Truly International: An American at Burghley

DENNY EMERSON

Hanging in my living room in Vermont is a montage of the American team at Burghley in 1974. Writing about that event three and one half years later, I find that memory, too, creates a montage, selecting and embellishing certain incidents that taken altogether form the fabric of the larger picture.

To help 'outsiders' understand the American Burghley expedition it is necessary to confirm some of the beliefs about our uniformity and precision of approach, but to tear away any mystery behind that approach. The system is simplicity in itself, and it centres around one outstanding coach who organised the training and conditioning routine and who in all other ways 'ran the whole show'.

There was once a famous American football coach named Vince Lombardi whose teams won championships year after year. All the sportswriters agreed that his teams didn't do anything that different or more dramatically than the other teams, but that they did the basics very, very well. Jack Le Goff is a Vince Lombardi. He is, as we say over here, a hard nosed S.O.B. when he trains his riders. He works through constant repetition, is tough on the riders (but not on the horses) and is very tough on himself. Picture the maestro of a symphony orchestra. As he conducts, he listens and can 'feel' the nuances and tonal qualities he is trying to draw from the musicians. This high intensity approach to teaching (typically Gallic, we might say) must for the instructor be enervating and frustrating to the point of rage. But it worked for the riders who could realise that it wasn't personal, although even then a 'one to one' session with Jack was almost more fraught with tension than actual competition!

Once, all six of us were at Wylye, our pre-World Championships headquarters, practising a simple dressage test on our second string horses prior to the Dauntsey Park event. Don Sachey remembered his test, but then Beth Perkins forgot a movement in hers. Small blow up from Jack. Then Bruce Davidson and Caroline Treviranus did theirs correctly. Then Mike Plumb made a mistake. 'Mike! We are supposed to be serious guys; you are the captain etc., etc.' Then I made a mistake, the third out of six. 'God for damn!' Slam! (his walking stick on to the ground). Aargh! (unintelligible), Slam! (his hat). Then about five minutes of tirade with my five buddies snickering and smirking out of Jack's sight, glad that I was getting it, not they.

This is not to say that all our training was painful confrontation, but there was a constant awareness of pressure and urgency that somehow (and I am not sure how) made us want to work harder, do better, and help each other, where it might so easily have worked the opposite effect. If there is a phrase that for me sums up Jack's teaching (and hence our uniformity of approach, I suppose) it would be 'constant, meticulous attention to detail'.

Our horses were a constant worry as we had no depth and lots of age. Furtive and Plain Sailing were fifteen, Good Mixture twelve, Victor Dakin and Cajun were eleven, and Irish Cap was the little kid at ten. I think the British riders and prognosticators from the equine press really had no clue as to the true American form, as we had been definitely ordered by Jack to stay under wraps at Charnock Richard, Stanton and Osberton, our three warm-up events. Our goal was always to try to get to Burghley with six sound horses.

Ironically, much of the spectacle of a huge event like Burghley is lost on the competitors themselves, immersed in their own tight little world of the stable area, the hotel, and the course. Every day that last week we were either schooling in dressage, taking a last stadium school or last gallop in a huge flat wheat field above Burghley House, or walking the course. For me there was the continuation of the running regimen that I had set for myself back on the chalk hills of Wylye, now carried out in a great level field across the road from the stables. I don't know whether it was the flat terrain, my increasing fitness or the absence of clinging wet chalk on my feet, but suddenly I found I could run for ever, and for the first time experienced a trace of that floating feeling of freedom from the body that is the special world of the conditioned athlete.

As the week of waiting ended, I would say that as a team we were cautiously optimistic. Beth Perkins broke her foot when a tack trunk fell on it, and although she could still ride, Jack left her off the team, opting for the less reliable Plain Sailing (whose over-aggressive jumping had been causing him to fall sometimes) but whose rider was fully sound.

We had three good dressage horses, Irish Cap, Furtive, and Cajun, and three not so good, Plain Sailing, Good Mixture, and my own Victor Dakin. About Victor and dressage, let me just say this. If Victor should die and be reincarnated as a dog, it will be as a small, noisy, quarrelsome Jack Russell terrier. That about sums up his approach to and performance in that discipline! Be that as it may, the team ended dressage in a strong position, but important as dressage may be, the cross-country is always the critical issue at any big event.

On the morning of Burghley show jumping I taped an interview for the

(Left) Denny Emerson and Victor Dakin.

(Right) Some of the American contingent during the World Championships in 1974. Among them are Neil Ayer, at far left; Jack Le Goff (arms folded); Mike Plumb, Denny Emerson and Bruce Davidson (far right).

United States Combined Training Association Magazine, regarding the cross-country I had jumped the day before. Referring to that subsequent article, I find that it tells the story with an immediacy that later reflections would have lost.

■ Two of the big differences I noticed eventing in the US and England were the size of the field of entries and the speeds at which the British compete. Where we would have a field of sixty entries at an event in both the Preliminary and Intermediate Divisions combined, the British would have over two hundred and sixty horses! To win an event in England you must really go fast. Their Novice Division, which is comparable to our Preliminary Division, is the lowest recognised level offered in England. At this level their required speed for cross-country is 525 metres per minute, compared to our 520. At the Intermediate and Advanced levels, the speed is 600 m.p.m., faster than that of International competition which is 570 m.p.m. The British really chase horses and, except at the high levels, you see some wild riding. They bring their young horses along quickly. A horse is quite likely to start at Novice this year and compete at Advanced the next.

In England the courses vary tremendously as they do in the United States. I had thought that all English courses would be beautiful; some were, like Sheila Willcox's and Osberton, but some were not. They have the same sort of problems we have here . . . too small rails, too sharp turns and bad footing. But, the big events are simply spectacular!

Burghley has the most ideal setting imaginable: rolling countryside, beautiful turf and wide-open vistas. The turns are big and sweeping and competitors are able to see the obstacles from a long way away. It is an excellent course for galloping.

There is no doubt about it, in 1974 the Burghley cross-country course was massive and nothing that I've done in the USA or Canada prepared me psychologically to jump anything that big. This course never let up on you from the third fence on. It kept hitting you with questions. At one obstacle you might be asked to jump out into space and then at the next to take back at an 18 ft. combination, next sail over a 6½ ft. wide, almost 4 ft. high oxer. The British riders compete at Badminton and Burghley every year and are well-accustomed to the scope of a course like this. Now, having done it, and the dragon's teeth have been pulled a little, it doesn't seem that bad.

This was a very fair course, however. You could get at every fence. There were some alternative fences that asked questions. The difficult ones were the obstacles where the ground gave way in front of the fence and where there was an impressive drop on the far side. There was never an easy choice. No matter where you jumped it, you had to stand back and fly out over the rails. If you didn't, you went down or stopped. You really had to ride forward.

PHASE A: The roads and tracks is little over 6 kilometres, and I must do 1 kilometre every 4 minutes. I also want to do about 1 minute at about 400 m.p.m. in order to do what Jack says—'put them on their legs a little bit'—get them ready to gallop. So we start out through the deer park next to the start of cross-country and head through a big stone gate into some woods through some rather rocky footing, to the top of a hill. After about 2 kilometres we come on to some good footing on a nice long track through

Mike Plumb and Good Mixture jump the Zig-Zag Rails. They finished less than a point behind the winners.

the woods. He's nice and relaxed so I pick up my canter here which puts me quite a bit ahead of my time. We now come to some dirt roads next to the Bull Pens, No. 16 and 17. I can see the huge crowds all over the cross-country course. I thought I might be nervous but fortunately I don't seem to get very much so anymore. Looking at my watch again I can see I am now about 2 minutes early reaching the box at steeplechase, so we just walk around and wait. Fortunately, Victor isn't nervous and doesn't pull a 'Plain Sailing', who stands up. He's quite good and relaxed, which is a pleasant change from one of our earlier events, Osberton, where he was quite bad. The loud speakers had really upset him there.

STEEPLECHASE: The 2 mile course is situated on the Burghley golf course. In order not to incur penalty points we must finish in 5 minutes 30 seconds. The idea is to check my watch at the first lap to see if I have done it in 2 minutes 45 seconds. Well, listening to the countdown, we are off. Its a long looking mile ahead and we must go around twice. Victor is galloping and jumping well, and checking my watch, I see that we are just about on the nose 2.45. As we start on the second lap, where we head down a small hill, Victor suddenly feels funny . . . he just isn't galloping as smoothly as before. I think he stung himself over the last fence or hit himself, so I let up on him a bit—slow down, and thank goodness his stride starts to feel even again. For a moment I have the awful thought, 'my gosh, maybe he's hurt himself!' What a terrible feeling. Well now he is going again, but he is tired. He just doesn't have the zip that he had the first go round. He is a little bit of an unknown quantity as he never had done a big three-day event like this before. This is the first 2 mile steeplechase he has ever done.

When you are riding on the team, each person on the team has specific orders. My orders with Victor were to feel him out, see how much he had, and most important—get around clear. You have four people going and if you can get the first two around clear, or with not too much trouble, then the Coach, Jack, is in a better position to send the other two riders on a bit and go for better time. When Victor started to get tired on the second lap, I took back, also, because I wanted to be sure I had enough horse left for the cross-country course.

45

Denny Emerson and Victor Dakin clear the Waterloo Rails. Five competitors fell at this fence, but Victor Dakin was one of the few horses who did not even touch it.

PHASE C: The land is flat with good footing, the temperature not too hot. Now that the steeplechase is finished, I want to give Victor a breather. The best way to do this is to get off and walk beside him. As part of our training we must jog at least a mile each day, so that I'm ready to jog beside him if need be. We walk along this way for about three minutes so that he can recover. I will have to catch up and be on my correct time by the middle of roads and tracks by cantering. I pop back in the saddle and Victor falls into a nice swinging rhythm at the trot, and shortly we pick up a canter to make up for the walk earlier.

He has come back quickly after our walk. I thought he was really tired after the steeplechase. Also I think he is a trifle overweight. Jack realised about two weeks ago that Victor was slightly heavier than he would have liked, but you can't do much galloping then because you stand a chance of hurting him. Victor is sort of an unknown quantity, he's a non-thoroughbred and had never done anything quite like this before. He hasn't been at the team very long, either. Well, the time has gone by faster than I thought it would and we are on our way to the box for the Vet Check and the start of Phase D. Jack is there.

PHASE D: Jack is in the box where I am headed for the vet check before the start of the cross-country. He is to tell me what the other riders have done and how the team stands. He says that Don has had a fall on Plain Sailing, and Beth Perkins on Furtive has gone clear. Beth's score doesn't count for the team, because she is competing as an individual. This makes a difference, as the individual can go-on a bit and do his own thing, but the team rider must follow specific orders which will benefit the team as a whole. With Victor the main thing is to get around the course clear, and not too slowly. The ten minutes in the box flies by awfully quickly. And before I know it I'm back up in the saddle for the countdown. So we are off again as Victor starts on the 14th mile of the endurance phase.

46

We gallop down to the 1st fence which is a big wagon with a log—not very high. I want to get Victor going forward and jumping 'already-going-forward' or what the British call 'attacking the fences'. He jumps it well and nicely in balance.

No. 1 Timber Wagon *Height 3 ft. 9 in. (1·07 m)*

We proceed on down a long lane lined with people on both sides, and then cross a road and press on down to a wooden wall. This is a straightforward fence, a nice warm-up, and we are over it easily.

No. 2 Wooden Wall *Height 3 ft. 9 in. (1·07 m)*

This chair-type obstacle is very big and very wide with maximum spread. It was constructed of wooden slats that made me think that a horse, if he chose to bank it, could easily get a leg down through the slats. This fence starts to set the tone of the course—big fences with big spreads. We drift up so that we get a fairly straight shot at it and he jumps it really galloping nicely forward.

No. 3 Lambert's Sofa *Height 3 ft. 10 in (1·17 m) Base spread 6 ft. 10 in. (2·08 m)*

Galloping along over the beautiful turf lanes which are formed by ropes holding back the crowds, I can see fence No. 4 just ahead. Here we swing around to the left and then back to the right for a straight approach to the easy alternative which is the single rails. We lose a little time doing this, but its not worth risking anything.

No. 4 Post and Rails *Height 3 ft. 9 in.–3 ft. 11 in. (1·07 m– 1·20 m) Top spread nil to 6 ft. 5 in. (1·90 m)*

We continue on hardly noticing the crowds which I was told later were about 80,000 on the cross-country. We are heading down a hill and just ahead lies the Double Coffin. After the first stock-ade fence the ground drops down and there are two ditches and then a very steep bank before the last fence. Princess Anne had a stop here at the out as Goodwill got under it and couldn't get out. I don't want him to be able to stop, coming into the first element by looking over it so I keep his head up, sit up a bit and keep my lower legs well on him. Now, as we land I look up at the escape hatch, the out, at the top of the hill. I don't worry what he does over the two ditches—he's very agile—I just ride for the out and he runs up the bank and pops out over the top.

No. 5 Double Coffin *Height 3 ft. 5 in.–3 ft. 11 in. (1·05 m– 1·20 m) Ditches 5 ft. and 5 ft. 6 in. (1·52 m and 1·68 m)*

No. 6 Lapped Rails *Height 3 ft. 11 in. (1·20 m)*

Then we swing left-handed and we run down to the next fence which has a little bank in front of it—he is so handy—that he jumps up on to this bank and is up and over the fence and we are away again.

No. 7 Sloping Rails *Height 3 ft. 7 in. (1·10 m) Base spread 8 ft. (2·44 m)*

On the course-walking I felt that this fence would set a tone as it requires the bold yet clever horse. It consists of sloping rails out of a poor approach. Coming down a little hill, it flattens out with about only one stride and then you have to shoot forward. Victor likes to come down to his fences and check himself, and then jump. On this kind of fence you can't do this. So I chase Victor into it and he answers by jumping boldly over it, and up on to the bank on the far side.

No. 8 Log Pile *Height 3 ft. 11 in. (1·20 m) Top spread 6 ft. (1·83 m)*

The Log Pile is another big fence, so I decide this is the moment to test him on this kind of fence. So I don't check him at all except to remind him that the fence is coming up and he sails over it in fine style. Now, I start to think I'm going to have a good round as he is jumping really boldly. It's a little early to think this I suppose but that's the feeling I have. My biggest worry is that he might run out of gas.

No. 9 Stockade *Height 3 ft. 2 in. (0·95 m) with drop*

Galloping on, we are now approaching the Stockade. This is a drop on to the road. Well, he doesn't hesitate and pops over it, down the bank on to the road and up the bank on the other side. He really has lots of spring.

No. 10 Park Gates *Height 3 ft. 11 in. (1·20 m)*

Now we head down a long hill and swing to the right. I don't check him much at all, just sort of set him. Victor always checks himself; he comes into this fence, does a quick-check and clears this simple straightforward gate with no problems.

We now wind up a long hill towards the Dairy Farm Rails. At this point I want to see how much horse I have left. This is what Jack calls 'listening to the motor'. So, I ask Victor to go forward, which he does. But, he does not 'spurt' forward, so I know I have to back off a bit. There is still a long way to go and I want to make sure I will have enough horse to finish with. We are now about one-third the way around the course and have gone over 1¼ miles. There are still almost 3 miles to go. Well, we head up to the rails which has a very steep approach, and he pops up and out over it very handily.

No. 11 Dairy Farm Rails (on to bank) *Height 3 ft. 8 in.* (*1·12 m*)

Now we swing left. This is one of the fences that I have been worried about. It consists of a big bank that slopes down with a big fence out in front of it, plus a 6-foot drop. Jack had told us to ride that fence as though there was no bank there, and when you are in the air, to sit back a bit, so that the horse can get his landing gear down. As we approach it, I can feel Victor doing his 'Victor Dakinshuffle'. As I said, he likes to come to a fence, shift his feet which gives him time to have a look at it, and then go. So I reach back and go to the bat, which scares the 'shuffle' out of him. Well, he just sails out into space like a rocket and lands just fine. What a nifty horse! I had heard before starting the cross-country that several horses had had problems at this fence.

No. 12 Dairy Farm Rails (off bank) *Height 2 ft. 9 in.* (*0·84 m*) *Drop 6 ft.* (*1·83 m*)

I'm feeling great as we approach the big Lamb Creep. We head on at the fence and sure enough Victor banks it. He pops his feet down behind, just as I figured he might as he did this same thing at Ledyard last year. Fortunately he never seems to slip down it—he's exceptionally clever with his feet.

No. 13 Lamb Creep *Height 3 ft. 10 in.* (*1·17 m*) *Base spread 8 ft. 6 in.* (*2·59 m*)

The land is generally quite flat and I'm not pressing him. I'd say we are galloping at about 520–530 m.p.m. I'm still concerned with having enough horse left to finish. The Sleeper Table is another one of the big oxers which this course features. It rides well for Victor. At these big oxers Victor doesn't do his 'shuffle' because this is the kind of fence that tells the whole story. He only does it when he cannot quite see what's there. He has a great regard for his own well-being and doesn't like to hit a fence one bit. In a 3-Day horse this is a trait that you have to stifle a bit.

No. 14 Sleeper Table *Height 3 ft. 8 in.* (*1·12 m*) *Top spread 6 ft. 6 in.* (*1·91 m*)

Before I know it we are over the Hayrack which is very straightforward. He has jumped it very nicely. Now I start thinking of my approach to the next combination.

No. 15 Hayrack *Height 3 ft. 11 in.* (*1·20 m*) *Top spread 6 ft. 2 in.* (*1·87 m*)

49

No. 16 and 17 Bull Pens *Height 3 ft. 9 in.–3 ft. 11 in.*
(1·07 m–1·20 m) Top spread nil or 4 ft. 6 in.–5 ft. 6 in.
(1·37 m–1·68 m)

No. 18 Sunken Wall *Height 3 ft. 10 in. (1·17 m)*

No. 19 Steps Down and Up *Height 3ft.–3ft. 10 in. (0·91 m–
1·17 m)*

No. 20 Hanging Log *Height 3 ft. 11 in. (1·20 m)*

No. 21 Birch Fence *Height 4 ft. 5 in. (1·34 m) Base spread
9 ft. (2·74 m)*

Now we run on down towards the Bull Pens which is a sort of a maze. We decide earlier that we would do this as three separate fences, instead of trying to jump the corner to save time, which is very risky indeed. So we come down to a collected canter, turn right, jump in, stop, turn left, jump out, turn right, and jump out again. All six of our horses did it this way and all six of them went through fine. Victor hits the 'out' because as we turn right I chase Victor to the bottom of the 'out'. This is a mistake. He isn't able to set himself up as he usually does and he hits the fence in front and pecks on landing but is O.K.

There is quite a dip in front of the Wall and the bank runs right up afterwards. The Wall rides very well as Victor is very nimble and probably has an easier time than some of the big horses.

We press on and make a U-turn into the Steps Down and Up. This is Victor's cup of tea—his footwork is quick and agile and he just jumps in, takes a stride, jumps down, takes a stride at the bottom, jumps up and takes a stride out over the rails. He seems to know where he is every second.

Running on, we cross a road and head into the Hanging Log which is maximum height, and which could give a tired horse a problem. Fortunately we sail over it and I start thinking about the Birch Fence coming up next.

This is a big fence, indeed, being 4 ft. 5 in. in height, and 9 ft. at the bottom. Well, ole Victor banks it, pops his feet down on it and keeps right on going. At this point the engine is still running well, I'm not chasing him, but trying to keep him in a rhythm. I'm beginning to think we had a good chance to go clear barring any accidents. He is jumping everything as though he really means it.

The water in the troughs is recirculated and squirts into each side through a little spout. None of the horses seem to take any notice of this. Victor jumps it in good form. Now I start to think seriously about the next fence that is coming up. It is one of the more difficult ones on the course.

The Waterloo Rails turned out to be well-named as it was, or almost was, the Waterloo for several horses. This is another one of those bank alternatives that slopes off before the fence with an enormous drop afterwards. The bank is all lumpy and uneven. We had decided to take the longer approach around to the left. I knew Victor would have to forget his 'shuffle' and stand off and jump, which happily for me, he does and doesn't catch a leg. It seems a long way down. We had dinner with the fence judge that evening and he said Victor was one of the very few horses who didn't hit this fence front or behind.

Riding on down around the edge of some small woods we turn right-handed into the water, which if you chose to lose time, you could just jog into. Victor gallops on down to it and steps in the far side. We are off again.

This combination is a good one for Victor as it is only 18 feet between the wall and the bank. He jumps in, takes a quick stride and is out. Plain Sailing, unfortunately had a little problem here by jumping in too big.

Moving on we come to a good long hill which leads down into the Trout Hatchery. This isn't the 'bugaboo' they say it is for nothing! You come down a long hill, the horses are tired, and it's near home. There is a funny little mound that you ride up on to, and then there is a steep slope. It's muddy and you are jumping into water. The rails stand straight at you, and the horse can see up straight through. The crowds are everywhere! I wanted Victor to jump off the bank not bury himself under the fence. Also you can't come in too fast, otherwise the horse might fall on landing in the water. We come in slowly but well in hand. Victor does stand off and lands in the water, and pops out over the log. Princess Anne almost came off here. There were several spectacular falls from horses getting buried under the fence and then going from there. André Le Goupil on Arthémise, who came to Ledyard last year, sadly was eliminated here.

No. 22 Water Troughs *Height 3 ft. 9 in. (1·07 m) Top spread 5 ft. 6 in. (1·68 m)*

No. 23 Waterloo Rails *Height 3 ft. 4 in.–3 ft. 7 in. (1·01 m– 1·09 m) Drop 6 ft. 6 in. (1·91 m)*

No. 24 Open Water *Spread 13 ft. (3·96 m)*

No. 25 Sleeper Wall and Bank *Height 3 ft. 8 in.–3 ft. 10 in. (1·12 m–1·17 m)*

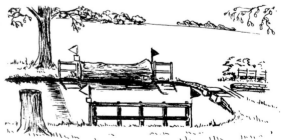

No. 26 and 27 Trout Hatchery *3 ft. 3 in. and 3 ft. 9 in. (1·00 and 1·15 m)*

No. 28 Zig-Zag Rails *Height 3 ft. 11 in. (1·20 m)*

No. 29 Birch Fence *Height 3 ft. 11 in. (1·20 m)*

No. 30 Double Rails *Height 3 ft. 11 in. (1·20 m) Top spread 6 ft. 6 in. (1·91 m)*

No. 31 Trakehner *Height 3 ft. 10 in. (1·17 m) Base spread 8 ft. (2·44 m)*

No. 32 The Raleigh Chopper *Height 3 ft. 9 in. (1·07 m) Top spread 5 ft. 4 in. (1·62 m)*

Moving on up the hill, we head for the Zig-Zag Rails. This, like the Dairy Drop earlier, was another fence that I was concerned about. It consists of a big ditch with a zig-zag over it, with rails 3 ft. 11 in. The approach is downhill into it, at an angle with a big ditch to jump plus an up bank on the far side. So it has height, spread, downhill and angle, near the end of the course. This is the kind of fence you must ride right on down to without checking. If you start looking and checking, you are inviting a stop or a fall. We had determined a specific line. So around the corner we come. We pick our line, I steady him and he stands off and jumps it very well. Victor is really great.

At this point, although I haven't been pressing on too much, I fortunately have some horse left. There is still that big third from the last fence to go. Also quite a good gallop on down to the next fence—slightly downhill. The Birch is big, which is good as it sets Victor up again and gets him jumping something that stands up in front of him —in preparation for the next fence which is impressive.

Victor has gone almost 17 miles now, as we head towards fence No. 30. This obstacle is large with maximum height and a 6 ft. 6 in. spread. It's built out of solid big poles yet it's airy. Coming across this long field, as we are about twenty strides away, I set him up a bit, by taking a little more hold of him, and drive him into my hands. He bounds over it.

It could be a bit premature, but I now feel we are home, as the next fence is a straightforward trakehner which should be no problem, but then you never know. This oft-times is where the problems arise when you get too confident. Anyway, we gallop straight on at it and Victor really flies over it. Later I heard this is where Columbus ridden by Mark Phillips, pulled his Achilles tendon when he dragged a hind leg over the log. He was withdrawn after cross-country, which was a real shame as he was standing in first place.

Up one little hill, there is not too much of a gallop into the Raleigh Chopper. I never thought a 'guillotine' could look so good. He sails on over it, and we run on in to the finish. Victor has some engine left, but not a whole lot.

We have some time penalties, but the most important thing is that Victor went clear and has been able to handle a course of this magnitude. He's a super little horse. ■

On the morning of show jumping, after learning of Columbus's withdrawal, we knew that virtually all we had to do to win the Team event was to avoid getting eliminated. However, all was not well behind our stall doors, either. Plain Sailing had a big haematoma on his belly from a fall at the Sleeper Wall and Bank, Good Mixture had landed on the landing side lip of the open water, and Victor had a very suspicious looking tendon, which I believe to have come from a rap or mis-step on the steeplechase when I felt him falter.

In other words, three of the four team horses were not 'sound' after cross-country and it became the task of the grooms and Allen Leslie the team veterinarian, who had worked for two years after vet school studying physical therapy on human athletes, to get them sound for show jumping. I won't go into the philosophical questions of whether top level international competition is often too hard on horses, but suffice it to say that an excellent veterinary surgeon like Allen Leslie or Peter Scott-Dunn is an essential ingredient of a team effort!

Allen and the grooms worked all night on the two legs with ice, and on the haematoma with an ingenious 'girdle' made of sacks and surcingles filled with ice, so that by the veterinary check the next morning the three horses were serviceably sound. In fact, the only one of the three to suffer longer term effects was Victor, who that fall had the tendon operation and a subsequent year off.

The show jumping itself was not so much a contest between teams as between Bruce Davidson, Mike Plumb and Hugh Thomas for the individual gold, silver and bronze medals. The American team was so far ahead after Columbus's withdrawal that even with a rail down by Plain Sailing and an uncharacteristic three rails down by an ailing Victor, the United States still won the team gold over Great Britain by 170 points. But only eight-tenths of one point separated the top three! In a way, they should all have won a gold medal; they are all great horses, but since none had a rail down, Bruce, Mike and Hugh finished in that order.

And so the United States made a 'clean sweep', its first major international victory in Three-Day Eventing since the Olympics of 1948. Was it a great triumph of one system over the others? Possibly. Of a better group of horses and riders over the others? Not at all, really. I have always remembered a quote in a book by Bill Steinkraus which says in effect 'When you do well, people praise you too highly; when you do poorly, people condemn you too greatly.' I think that the American Burghley expedition was a carefully planned, meticulously prepared campaign, backed by hundreds of supporters, that happened to 'click' at the right place and time. None of us would say that with a little shifting of luck it mightn't have gone another way, but this time, at Burghley, it didn't, and it was great fun to have been a part of it all.

*Members of the FEI
Bureau at Burghley for
the first World
Championships in 1966.
From left: Colonel
Nyblaeus (Sweden),
Brigadier J. Grose, Mr
Pedro Mayorga
(Argentina), Mr
Devereux (USA),
General Stoytchev
(Bulgaria), Mr Wylie
(Eire), the Marquess of
Exeter, Colonel Bruni
(Italy), Mr Sarasin
(Switz.), Chevalier de
Menten de Horne
(Belgium), E. Graf
Rothkirch (Germany),
Sir Henry Tate,
Captain Clavé (France)
and Mr Bill Thomson.*

*(Below) From France:
Adjutant Le Goff and
Laurier, 1963 (3rd).*

TRULY INTERNATIONAL

(Left) *From West Germany: Horst Karsten and Sioux, 1977 (3rd).*

(Below, left) *From Ireland: John Watson and Cambridge Blue, 1977 (6th).*

(Below, right) *From the USSR: Gazjumov and Granj, 1962 (2nd).*

'Come on England, Come on George'

LUCINDA PRIOR-PALMER

He was a brilliant horse. He had won Badminton five months before in superior and exemplary fashion. He arrived at Burghley four days before the European Championships were due to begin. He seemed a little bored, almost dull. I could not give him spark. There was a temporary void of life in me, too. I felt ill and slept each and all afternoon. I walked the cross-country very early in the morning before the crowds arrived, and before I might start to feel peculiar again. The course did not inspire me, but then I felt that is was probably my fault not the course's. None of it really frightened me enough to ensure that I rode my best. On the other hand, the very fact that I was *not* worried rendered me sufficiently respectful of it.

Friday was Dressage Day. At 7.15 am, Colonel Bill Lithgow picked me up and drove me from the *George* Hotel to the cross-country course. (It had been on St *George's* Day, that *George* had won Badminton.)

For the third and final time I walked every blade of grass that I hoped George would tread. Occasionally I recalled interviews with English and European journalists, which during the last few days, had served to remind me that I was in fact defending my European Championship title. Normally it is a fight to push away such pressurising thoughts. This time it was no problem. They slipped back into the dimness of my unimpassioned mind as easily as they had escaped.

Over half of the course was walked as I wandered down the slope from the Hayrack. On the right stretched the great lake, at one end of which stood the turreted baroque fairy-castle, Burghley House. For a moment the burden lifted. I felt happy. In the water of the lake the early morning sun reflected the bluest of skies. No-one else was about. There was no sound. Surrounded by the benevolent strangeness of the park's ancient oak trees I felt a sense of genuine pride. Here, in England, a country for which people often make apologies to their visitors, was an immovable relic of the glorious, invincible heritage which we British enjoy. For several minutes I stood still, absorbing the peace and the magnificence. The complications of walking the cross-country course for the European Championships shrank proportionately when compared to the skills of the men who had fashioned such beauty.

I squelched on. My gym shoes had been soaked through since Fence 3, the Leaf Pit. The dew within them had warmed to blood temperature around my feet. They felt like a pair of thermally insulated shock absorbers. (On the first day, walking in rubber boots had produced instant blisters.)

George felt dull that morning. His owner, Mrs Straker, advised me not to school him but to take him instead for a gay 'hunting' ride. We galloped

across stubble fields, leaped hedges, popped over rails. George jumped cleanly and cheerfully. An hour later a happy horse waltzed back to his stable. He ate his lunch and Lisa began his hairdressing session. Meanwhile I changed into top-hat, tail coat, breeches and boots, pondering all the time what to do with George before his test. It seemed that, in contrast to any other horse I had ever ridden, he was going to require livening up for his dressage. I was not quite sure, however, what sort of electrifying effect the arena might have on him. I had a suspicion that such was his mood at that moment that he would not notice whether he was surrounded by a packed grandstand or a thicket of trees. I took a chance and left him in his stable until twenty minutes before his test.

With girths tightened but stirrups at long dressage length I set sail from the stable area at a strong canter and pointed George at a couple of practice cross-country fences and a show-jump. As I flashed through the park perimeter gate and cantered up towards the main arena, I caught sight of my (recently widowed) mother laughing out loud to herself. I suppose it *was* an amusing sight: tail coat flying, hand on top-hat to anchor it, as George leaped big solid timber fences.

After ten minutes of small circles and transitions under the eye of Spanish Riding School artist Ernst Bachinger, George cantered quietly into the ring. He definitely noticed that the grandstand housed people and not trees. He became a little more lively: enough for me to ride him with impulsion but not enough to prevent me from hurrying him in an attempt to make him appear more active. I had not noticed much in those two days of dressage, but I *had* appreciated that the judges had marked an accurate but dull test very poorly. This was what I feared George would present—hence the jumping beforehand to return to him some of the zest he had shown in the spring.

The test did not seem brilliant, because George did not feel as supple and submissive as he might. Maybe my nerves had tensed me against him and prevented him from giving through his whole body. However, it must have looked better than it felt. His score headed the twelve British competitors and he lay third overall. Karl Schultz and Madrigal were over 10 points ahead. A German lady was only a fraction of a point in front. Eyes and thoughts turned to the next day's decisive cross-country.

That evening the twelve British riders collected in the tented tack-room. With our new chief, Tadzik Kopanski, and with Richard Meade and Dick Stillwell, we discussed together how best to attack the course and its 33 fences. It was a helpful hour for some. Others were reduced to tears when, from the discussion, they discovered that they were the only one who was intending to take a fence at a certain place while everyone else thought their particular route was crazy.

I was confident that I knew what I was going to try and ask George to do on the cross-country. Just before supper, several of us drove to the steeplechase course for one final walkround. A few days earlier I had taken great pains to study this phase by walking it with Chris Collins, ex-champion amateur jump jockey, as my adviser. George was not a very fluent jumper of 'chase fences', and I had developed a time-consuming habit, at Burghley, of taking the wrong roped-off channel as I galloped round past the start to begin the second circuit.

The morning of cross-country day is not an easy one for the nerves. I do not like to walk the course, or parts of it, again, as I want to save all my energies for riding. George was not scheduled to start Phase A until 3 pm. There was a great deal of waiting to be done between breakfast and 3 o'clock. I have my own remedy for these long waits. This time I did not go to my hotel bed until midnight, and, despite a hopeful 'daily' coming into my room twice during the morning to make my bed, I did not wake up long enough to climb out until 11 o'clock. I dressed and wandered down to have some breakfast and to read the papers. No breakfast, no papers. Instead, I ordered a lump of cheddar cheese and—reckoning on the reviving powers of the beverage—a pot of tea, and took it back to my little bedroom.

I packed my cross-country clothes in a shoulder-bag and swung my crash-hat from the other arm. The queue of traffic outside the hotel was moving more slowly than I was walking, as it snailed its way towards the great walls of Burghley Park. So much for my energy-saving routine. I was going to have to walk the mile down to the stables.

George was already plaited, although he still had three-quarters of an hour before he was due to be tacked up. He looked well enough, but drowsy and somewhat disinterested. I wondered if he felt any better than I did. I hoped so.

At exactly 3 o'clock, weighed out and suitably equipped, George and I started on the first leg of the speed and endurance phase of the 1977 European Championships. During the following $1\frac{1}{2}$ hours I began to understand for the first time why this phase of the Three-Day Event is so named.

George finished Phase A sweating. It was not a hot day, but his sides heaved already as he stood quietly at the start of the steeplechase. (What a change from my 1975 European Champion Be Fair. His nerves had always caused him to fidget about on his hind legs at the start.) It crossed my mind to wonder if George was as healthy as he ought to be.

The first two fences felt good. George seemed safer and more sure of his jumping than he had done on the Badminton steeplechase. He was holding his neck and head in a fairly high position and jumping off his hocks. He rounded the turn at the far end and gradually began to lose his style. His head and neck lowered, his rhythm altered as he lumbered along on his forehand. He felt a little tired already, and we had been barely one quarter of the way. He jumped the next three fences up the straight in such mediocre fashion that I wished there were not another entire circuit still to come. He began to lean on the left rein, a habit he had always fostered but which worsens as he tires. He rounded the sharp turn at the top of the course and galloped, head low, towards the roped-off channels, one of which formed the beginning of the second circuit. How I wished that it were the end. George felt tired. I was already dead beat. As we thundered down between the ropes, George leaning hard left, I must have shifted my weight, for in an instant he had moved a little to his left and tangled his galloping legs in the low-slung stringing. He tripped lower and lower with each stride until I was sure that he would somersault. But somehow he stayed upright. Instead I shot over his head into the air, and thudded to the ground. I clung to the reins as George galloped relentlessly on, dragging me along on my backside.

I remember being not in the slightest bit surprised. Somehow I had known for several hours that this day was going to be a disaster. Nothing had felt right. George hadn't. I hadn't. The atmosphere I had created for myself was all wrong. I bumped and bounced along the grass in between

those pounding front feet, which never once touched me. The awfulness of the situation seemed in keeping with the past weeks. I told myself simply 'You silly B . . . you knew you'd bog it but did you have to do it this early?'

Suddenly I realised that George didn't seem to have noticed that I was no longer on his back but around his feet. I always thought he had a hard mouth but I hadn't thought it could be insensitive enough to drag ten stone along without realising. It did not seem that he was going to stop galloping and we were heading for the turn. Somehow I had to remind him of my whereabouts. I cannot remember why, but for some reason I had to cross on my bottom in front of his speeding legs in order to be in a better position to attract his attention and to stop him. Suddenly he seemed to hear 'Whoah George, whoah', and felt a downward jog on the right-hand side of his mouth. He stopped quietly and quickly—apologetic at not having appreciated the situation earlier. He stood like a rock: 16·2 of big brown horse waiting to be remounted.

No-one rushed to give me a leg-up. Any spectator that I could see was standing open-mouthed, transfixed by what they were watching and consequently rooted to the ground. With a huge heave which drained the last ounce of my flagging energy I half scrambled and half vaulted into the saddle. George set off again, head low, hocks strung well out behind, leaning hard left.

To this day I do not know how he jumped that last circuit of five fences. I could do nothing to help him. I was as weak and useless as a sack of potatoes. When he was wrong for a fence he made no effort to shorten and to adjust his stride. Instead he used the ground-boards like step-offs as he ploughed through the fences. Galloping towards the open ditch, he was bearing so hard to port that I had to haul him back on course with both hands, lest he by-passed the fence altogether.

I remember being certain that he could not remain standing up if he continued jumping like that. I was sure that we would be over the time limit, although I had not dared to look at my stop-watch since I had fallen off: I was so sure that all was already lost. I felt sufficiently out of touch with things to entertain only one wish. I hoped that George would hurry up and fall and then I could become unconscious and be able to sleep and sleep and sleep . . .

He almost missed the finish. Pulling hard left, George thundered towards the second circuit channel once again, instead of the finish channel. I stole a glance at my stop-watch as I flicked it back to zero for the start of Phase C. It looked as if it said five minutes—but I did not believe my eyes. Five minutes was the time-limit. I was certain that we must be outside it, and that we had knocked up a score of time penalties.

For the next 8 kilometres I played alternately the roles of nurse and persuader, as George straggled along the Roads and Tracks slowly, oh so slowly, recapturing some of the strength and energy that he had expended during our hectic steeplechase. In the back of my mind I was not sure whether he was 100 per cent well, but there was nothing positive to prove my fractional suspicion.

We trotted into the 'Box'. Tadzik ran up smiling. 'Did you know? You're OK. No time faults on the steeplechase'.

No wonder poor George had taken so long to recover while on Phase C. He must have completed that second circuit half a minute faster than he should have done allowing for the time my fall had taken. Thankfully I handed him over to his team of well-ordered Nannies to wash him down and refresh him. Meanwhile I slumped into a striped plastic beach-chair and was quietly but firmly briefed as to how all the cross-country fences were jumping. I heard what they were saying, but I could barely keep my calm. Over $4\frac{1}{2}$ miles and 33 fences to come. Even if George had the strength left, I knew that I had not. And I knew that the more tired he was the heavier he would lean on me. I begged not to be informed of the score position. I did not want to know that the British team was relying on us for a good clear round. George and I would do our best, but I was not at all confident that our best would be good enough. I left my collapsible chair and wandered to the tented ladies loo. As I sat there I knew that there was nothing much left in me. Anything that happened now was entirely in the hands of my Maker. I asked His help.

George sprang over the first two fences with feet to spare: revelling in the power of his own jump. He lowered himself neatly down the drop into the depths of the Leaf Pit below. You don't hear much when you're riding, but the deafening roar of the patriotic crowd as he landed sent us on our way with renewed courage and strength. He jumped hard left over the next fence and rattled both parts of the ensuing double. I yelled down his ear that he really must pick his feet up a bit better than that over the next twenty-nine. He listened and co-operated, though he became momentarily straddled as he lost his footing when bouncing out over the rails of the half-coffin. He ate up the Irish Bank, the Trout Hatchery and the following four fences. He stood off an extra stride at the Troughs and I heard the gasp of the spectators. But George's limitless scope carried us out of trouble. I cursed myself for this near disaster as I had not gathered him together sufficiently before the fence. He took me over the next few fences, over the Hayrack down past the Lake and past the tree that I had leaned up against early the previous morning. He cantered up the Dairy Mound and popped over the Jubilee Table. No trouble, because no serious collecting up was needed.

The first of the fences which I feared most, was closing in on us. It was 3 ft. 8 in. high and it was at the summit of the steep bank into Capability's Cutting. Unfortunately it was approached off a downhill turn. It was that turn which I knew to be our problem. George would have preferred to canter straight on, continuing homewards. At the last moment he turned left-handed, answering my repeated demands, but he didn't notice any collection aids. Only because he is the bold horse that he is was he able to stumble and pop over those rails and down the bank. Any normal horse similarly uncollected and badly presented would have either stopped or fallen.

Three fences later came the second of my three worries. Another sharp turn into a post and rails set on the far side away from the lip of a bank and ditch. Without my usual strength, I found it impossible to gather him together. Once again he crashed across it, legs everywhere. Once again he saved the day. As we cantered up the slope towards the last little strip of wood I was glad that I had always agreed with Frank Weldon that men were preferable to women in teams, as they coped better with stress and strains. I think I would have cried and flopped off then and there, I felt so weak, but for an English country gentleman, who raised his shooting stick high in the air as George, head low and heavy, mouth dead, galloped by: 'Come on England, come on George.'

There was one more straightforward fence before the complications of the Double Coffin. George sailed effortlessly over it. All I could do to prepare him for the Double Coffin was to slow down by turning his face into the crowd. Using my voice to encourage him on again I turned him to face the palisade on the brink of the bank at whose base there was a double of ditches and a stride up another bank followed by a palisade out. Once more all praise to that incredible horse. He picked up his feet and leaped neatly over all four parts. The cheers of the spectators were deafening. George had earned it all and more. As for me—I have never felt less deserving of such support.

The final four fences were a formality to most. But four years earlier when ridden by his owner's son, Matthew Straker, George had had an ugly fall over the last but one, 'Lambert's Sofa'. I had to remind him as best I could not to do the same again. He remembered, and taking absolutely no risks—having courted disaster so intimately throughout the afternoon—we straightened up a long way back for the final fence, the Raleigh Bicycles wall. Thus George finished one of my least favourite speed and endurance tests with only 5·4 time faults, putting the British Team into a good lead and himself into second place individually, 9 penalties behind Karl Schultz and Madrigal.

George was washed down, made warm and comfortable and put to bed with a 'thank you' hug. I wandered across to where the Germans sat drinking beer on the grass outside their stables. We discussed each other's fortunes and failings. My friendly instincts soon surrendered to fatigue combined with intense relief. I flopped down for half an hour and lay stretched out on the ground, still wearing crash-hat and cross-country number. Eventually my body was persuaded to leave the grass and my boots my feet. Some kind person drove me back to the hotel. The *George*.

Attending the dance on cross-country night is for me an essential part of the Event. I feel that it is Phase E, and without it the speed and endurance has not been completed. For the first time in my life I failed to summon either the energy or the enthusiasm to attend the Burghley Ball that evening. Alone in my little bedroom I felt a profound gratitude to my Maker. There was no doubt that He had been working overtime that Saturday afternoon.

Sleep was no problem. The fact that I was within a fence of a second European Championship did not excite me. It barely occurred to me. In spite of Madrigal's dicey show-jumping ability I thought that he would go clear. I felt that Karl Schultz had ridden an excellent cross-country round and that therefore he deserved to win. I did not even feel justified in lying second, let alone winning.

All Sunday morning, Oliver Plum, my cavalier spaniel and constant companion, was left wandering pathetically around the car park of the George Hotel. I didn't notice his absence all day. Fortunately my mother did, and performed the necessary rescue. My mind was functioning with even less speed. I went to church during the morning and was twice left standing up on my own when the congregation was already on bended knee.

At Peter Scott-Dunn's private vet's inspection late the previous night, George had seemed none the worse for his exertions. After a good sleep he was perky and bright when we went for a gentle ride around the park in the morning. With his muscles suitably unstiffened he passed the official vet's inspection and went back to his stable for a little more rest until the Grand Parade at 2 o'clock.

But he was a tired horse. I warmed him up after the parade as gently and progressively as possible. He did not give me the same feeling of lightness and elasticity as he had done five months earlier at Badminton. He felt old, as if he no longer loved every step he trod. I jumped only a few practice fences. He was not making any effort to jump well. Either he knocked the pole down or he just skimmed across the top. I did not know what to do with him to ensure that he jumped the vital clear-round. But what I *did* know was that I must not continue practising. I walked him up to the stadium area with only one thin shred of confidence in our combined abilities to jump clear. I hoped that George would sense the occasion and make the effort in the arena that he was unwilling to make outside it.

Lisa led George round. With his pale blue Union-Jack-emblazoned rug thrown over his saddle and loins, he looked man enough. But his head was low and his feet dragged a little across the ancient turf. I went over to the arena to watch Schultz and Madrigal jump. I felt that George had had enough. I could see no reason why he should not go into that arena and knock five fences down, as apparently he had done a few years earlier.

Madrigal was jumping well. I found myself hoping that he would go clear: so that the pressure would be off George and me. It wouldn't then matter quite so much if we knocked a few down, since we would have had no chance for an Individual Gold anyway.

The penultimate fence rattled to the ground. Madrigal emerged with 10 penalties. George and I only had to clear twelve small fences to become European Champions. Only . . . *only* twelve fences. I knew it was twelve too many. I hung to my shred of confidence, hoping that through his innate intelligence George would sense the importance of the occasion and would react accordingly.

Five minutes before we were due to jump I re-mounted and Dick Stillwell helped us over a few practice fences. George jumped idly. Dick made the fence very big. George hit it hard. He came round again and jumped it better. He felt laboured, but he had tried. We stopped jumping and walked slowly around the collecting ring. Dick came over and gave my backside a painful pinch and said 'C'mon girl, what's up with you then? Will you please wake yourself up?' My mother had spotted the daze I was in and had mentioned it to Dick, knowing he would understand how best to cope with the situation.

Sioux and Horst Karsten were lying third. They cantered out of the arena with one fence on the floor. George walked towards the entrance. Dick delivered another nerve-awakening pinch. I smiled and trotted George into the arena.

Never have I been more grateful to the Great British Public. They roared as George came in. Their enthusiasm and their tension transmitted themselves instantly to my horse. He pricked his ears and threw out his toes as he floated in extended trot towards the Royal Box. We halted and saluted, and as we moved off into canter an extraordinary hush fell on the whole of the Burghley stadium.

How George ever jumped over the top of those twelve fences and not through the middle I do not know. I was sure that through his idleness and tiredness he would become careless if he met a fence 'right', so I encouraged him to come very close to the first six. He had to perform a series of gymnastic feats to get himself out of trouble. But he knew. He was determined not to knock anything. Gradually I relaxed a little and dared to ride him more 'forward', thereby making his task easier.

We squared up for the final fence—a red-brick wall. Earlier I had watched three out of six people knock a brick from the top of this wall. Would George flick one out too and lose everything? Or would he . . . ?

I couldn't stop the new European Champion as he ran away around the arena. The noise of the ecstatic home crowd went to both our heads. He galloped on, round and round, my febble pulls having no effect. But then they hadn't had much effect over the past three days, and yet George had still managed to clinch for Britain the European Team Title and to win for himself the Individual Gold Medal. He was a brilliant horse. I thought how pleased my father would have been, and hoped that he had been watching it all from his new front row seat in the skies.

64

The interest and excitement among spectators attending their first ever
Burghley Horse Trials were equally matched by anxiety behind the scenes.
No amount of careful planning could ordain the size of the crowds, and
there had been some uncertainty as to how many competitors could be
expected.

1961

    The organisers had sent invitations to eight nations, but with an inter-
national Three-Day Event scheduled to take place in Geneva shortly after
Burghley, entries from the Continent were not forthcoming. Initial
estimates that there would be as many as sixty competitors proved to be
over-optimistic, for in spite of the minimal qualifications—horse and rider
had to have completed only two open, unrestricted or intermediate classes
—entries closed with thirty-three on the list, and by 'D Day' they had been
whittled down to twenty.

    If the general standard of competitors was not impressive, there was one
star among them who soon made his presence felt. Mrs Gilroy's Merely-a-
Monarch, ridden by Anneli Drummond-Hay, performed a dressage test of
a quality only rarely seen in horse trials. A magnificent big dark brown
horse of enormous presence, he was a beautiful mover and had great
natural rhythm. He was only six years old and this was his first Three-Day
Event. At Tidworth earlier in the year he had completed the dressage but

had then been withdrawn, as the going had been exceptionally hard. But he had already attracted attention at the Horse of the Year Show the previous year, when he had won the Spiller's Combined Training Competition; and had finished 3rd in the final of the Foxhunter jumping. In the spring he had been a convincing winner of the intermediate class at Sherborne Horse Trials.

Anneli Drummond-Hay, then aged 24, was a highly respected rider. She had twice been 3rd at Badminton—in 1958 on Pluto, and in 1960 riding Perhaps, when she had been in the lead at the end of the second day, only to drop to 3rd with 20 show jumping penalties.

With a dressage score of 38, Anneli and Merely-a-Monarch established a lead of 26 points over their nearest rivals, Celia Ross-Taylor and King Midas. Third were Michael Bullen and Sea Breeze—a fancied combination as they had finished 4th at Badminton—and in 4th place were By Golly and Lieutenant Jeremy Smith-Bingham. The dressage test, the BHS Official Medium (Badminton) Test, included movements similar to those in later years—among them half-passes and counter-canter, but in addition it demanded pirouettes.

Bill Thomson had started work on his cross-country course in July expecting a substantial foreign entry, and some of the obstacles caused apprehension among the less experienced riders. For the first time, competitors were confronted by fences which are now familiar features of Burghley—the Maltings, Capability's Cutting, the Bull Pens and the Trout Hatchery. At the latter, competitors had a choice of jumping a log and landing in the water, or a post and rails with a drop set back from the water.

At a distance of $4\frac{1}{2}$ miles the course was slightly longer than is now customary for a CCI, and it went further in an easterly direction, beyond Two Lords. The steeplechase was sited in the deer park in the area south of the golf course between the two great double avenues of limes.

Wearing Number 1 was Lieutenant-Colonel Frank Weldon, riding Mr Neil Gardiner's Young Pretender. On the steeplechase they finished with 14 seconds in hand and set out on the cross-country at a great gallop. They went well until reaching Fence 23—a post and rails with a drop coming out of Chabonel Spinney—where they met with disaster. Weldon and Young Pretender disagreed about where they should take off: the horse put in an extra stride and took a crashing fall. Shaken but unhurt, Weldon remounted, and they still clocked the fastest time of the day to move up to 4th place.

Sea Breeze had been withdrawn after the dressage, as he was not fully fit. Another fancied combination, Norman Arthur riding O'Malley's Tango, on whom Anneli Drummond-Hay had won at Tidworth, was eliminated at Capability's Cutting. Following them, Janine Sebag-Montefiore and Samantha notched a total of 420 jumping penalties: a Burghley record which has stood the test of time!

There were other eliminations and retirements—among them Celia Ross-Taylor and King Midas—before Jeremy Smith-Bingham and By Golly accomplished the first clear round in a good time which took them temporarily into the lead. Patrick Conolly-Carew from Ireland, riding Ballyhoo, also completed a good round, marred only by a single refusal at Capability's Cutting, and at the end of the day they were lying 3rd.

The Trout Hatchery claimed two eliminations, three falls and several

refusals, and it put paid to the chances of another of the fancied entries: Cottage Romance and Michael Bullen, who had been 4th in the Rome Olympics and 3rd at Badminton in the spring.

Merely-a-Monarch was last to go, and Anneli knew that she had considerable leeway. She did not attempt maximum bonus on the steeplechase but put up a good time on the cross-country to return a clear round—only the second of the day. So the resounding lead that they had established in the dressage was just marginally diminished after the speed and endurance. By Golly, who was demoted to 2nd, had an advantage of no fewer than 82·4 points over Ballyhoo.

Ten of the nineteen horses which started out failed to complete the cross-country, and it was generally felt that the course had been too severe for the standard of entry.

It was predictable that the jumping would be unlikely to cause a major upset—for Merely-a-Monarch was already a Grade A show jumper. He duly completed an outstanding performance with a confident clear round, thus heading with his illustrious name the Burghley Roll of Honour. He was a horse who had so caught the public imagination that Anneli Drummond-Hay was invited to appear with him as one of the 'personalities' at the Horse of the Year Show, where he delighted the crowd by persistently trying to unseat his jockey.

1961. Anneli Drummond-Hay and Merely-a-Monarch fly the Open Water.

1962
EUROPEAN CHAMPIONSHIPS

In 1961 the competition at Burghley had been something of a dress rehearsal for the European Championships to be held here in 1962. This was to be Burghley's début as an International Three-Day Event, and the organisers took immense trouble with their preparations to ensure that everything would go smoothly.

Before the Event there were no clear favourites among the teams. In the 1959 European Championships at Harewood the British team had lost the title for the first time since the competition's inauguration at Badminton in 1953, having just been pipped by the Germans. But the Harewood form was unhelpful, as the Germans did not send a team to Burghley and there were no surviving British team horses of that year.

After winning at Badminton in the spring, Anneli Drummond-Hay had turned Merely-a-Monarch to show jumping—which added to the difficulties of the team selectors, as it deprived them of the one outstanding partnership. The final team trial at Eridge had resulted in a win for Captain James Templer and M'Lord Connolly. It was, however, their first international season, and having been eliminated in the French Championships at Fontainebleau they were not selected for the team but went to Burghley as first reserves.

The British team consisted of Colonel Frank Weldon on Neil Gardiner's Young Pretender, who had been second at Badminton; Susan Fleet on The Gladiator; Michael Bullen on Colonel Williams's Sea Breeze; and Captain Peter Welch on Mister Wilson, who had been 5th at Fontainebleau where the course had been very big.

The Russians were considered a danger. They brought over five horses, all very lean and hard and rumoured to have undergone a selection process so tough that it had broken down many horses. Attired in shocking-pink track suits, the riders had enjoyed a morning's cub-hunting with the Cottesmore a few days before the Event. Both the French and the Irish also fielded good teams—the latter included two generations of the Freeman-Jackson family, father and daughter.

In addition to the four international teams there were eleven English individuals who in order to qualify had been required to have won £15 in prize money and to have completed two intermediate horse trials.

For the dressage the FEI had devised a new test—the one that came into widespread use as the FEI Three-Day Event Test (1963). As expected, the Russians showed a distinct superiority in this phase. Sabaital Mursalimov, their reserve rider, took the lead on Sekret, and Boris Konjkov on Rumb went into 2nd place. M. le Roy of France and Garden, winners at Fontainebleau, were 3rd; 4th, 9 points behind the leader, were James Templer and M'Lord Connolly. Templer was able to ride the horse for only seven minutes before the test, for if he went on any longer M'Lord Connolly usually spoilt his test by constantly shaking his head. Satrap and Pavel Deev were 5th for the USSR, and 6th was the second British reserve, Jane Wykeham-Musgrave on Ryebrooks—a very big, good-looking horse and a former winner of the Working Hunter of the Year.

The British reserves fared better than the team, of which the best performance was by Sea Breeze (7th). Mister Wilson was 12th, The Gladiator 13th, and Young Pretender, who took a violent dislike to one of the corners of the arena and every time he was supposed to come to it shot off, paying scant regard to the movements of the test, was only third from the bottom, with a score of 113·5.

At the end of the dressage the Russians headed the team placings with a total of 196 for their best three. The French were not far behind with 203, Britain was 3rd with 223·5, and the Irish were 4th with 258. The multiplying factor—the amount by which the dressage scores are multiplied to give them the correct influence in relation to the cross-country—had been set at 1·5, which meant that it would be difficult for those who had performed badly in the dressage to overcome their disadvantage with good cross-country scores.

The cross-country was $4\frac{3}{4}$ miles, the steeplechase was $2\frac{1}{4}$ and the total distance of the speed and endurance test was $18\frac{3}{4}$ miles.

The course followed largely the track of the previous year, but there were many new fences. The President of the Ground Jury, Mr E. Sarasin from Switzerland, in his report to the FEI remarked on the 'astonishing variety of fences', and added that 'The "problem" fence, an interesting English speciality, giving the rider a choice of jumping the obstacle in different ways, was represented five times'.

1962, The European Championships. (Above) *Team Champions, the USSR:* (left to right) *Lev Baklyshkin and Khirurg (7th), Pavel Deev and Satrap (5th), Guerman Gazjumov and Granj (2nd) and Boris Konjkov and Rumb (15th).* (Below) *Individual Champions James Templer and M'Lord Connolly stand off the Saw Bench.*

69

Among Bill Thomson's cunningly devised 'problem' fences were the Waterloo Rails, where there was a choice of either big rails with a big drop, a very high gate or a post and rails on a bank. There was an interesting series of fences at the Bull Pens, where it was possible to save time by jumping wide parallels, or playing safe by going between the rails and jumping a stile at the end. Only four horses jumped the 6 ft. 4 in. spread, among them Sea Breeze and Young Pretender. At the Trout Hatchery there were some rails one stride in front of the water and a log in the middle of the water.

In spite of heavy rain in the morning and periodic showers throughout the day, the going was perfect. A British individual, Barbara Pearson riding Anna's Banner, was first to go and put up a fine performance to complete the course in a good time with only one refusal. But from the beginning things did not go well for the British team. First member of the team to go was Mister Wilson, and he was eliminated at the Sleeper Bank at the Maltings. Susan Fleet and The Gladiator had refusals at the Y Fence at Two Lords and the Waterloo Rails, and then a fall at the log in the Trout Hatchery; but to the admiration of the crowd, she remounted despite being soaked, and finished the course in reasonable time. Sea Breeze and Michael Bullen went brilliantly—fast and clear—until at the second from last fence, an innocuous log, Sea Breeze over-jumped, stumbled on landing and fell just inside the penalty zone. He still scored a maximum bonus (86) and in spite of the 60 penalties was lying 8th at the end of the day.

Last of the British team to go was Frank Weldon with Young Pretender. They completed a good clear round—but not at quite the consuming speed that spectators had come to expect of Weldon. Though they earned a bonus of 62·8 their dressage score proved an insuperable disadvantage, and in spite of their good cross-country they could only move up to 10th place.

Towards the end of the day sagging English morale received a boost with two very good performances from individuals. Ryebrooks, a great cross-country performer—'a horse in a million' according to his rider—made no mistakes in a superb round, and his bonus of 78·8 was good enough to put him in the lead at the end of the day. Following him, James Templer, who had run beside his horse to save its energy for almost the whole distance of the roads and tracks, kept up a relentless pace on M'Lord Connolly. But this was never an especially bold horse and he did not like water or ditches, and at the Trout Hatchery he had a refusal. He scored maximum bonus but the 20 penalties cost him the lead.

The Russians, to the surprise of everyone who thought that their light-framed horses would be unable to withstand the rigours of the cross-country, went extremely well. Guerman Gazjumov and the ten-year-old chestnut mare Granj scored maximum bonuses on both steeplechase and cross-country—the only combination to do so without incurring any jumping penalties—and at the end of the day they were lying 3rd. Khirurg and Lev Baklyshkin were also clear but lost time on the steeplechase; Satrap had one refusal at the Waterloo Rails; Rumb, with the best dressage score of the team, had a fall at the Timber Wagon and two refusals. The Russians had chosen their team wisely, for their reserve horse Sekret—the dressage star—was unable to cope with the cross-country and was eliminated at the Waterloo Rails.

The real heroes of cross-country day were the Irish. St Finbarr and Harry Freeman-Jackson, Sam Weller and Anthony Cameron, and

Ballyhoo and Patrick Conolly-Carew all jumped clear and all earned good bonus scores. But with the exception of St Finbarr, who was lying 6th at the end of the day, their poor dressage scores kept them well down the order. For Virgina Freeman-Jackson it was not a happy occasion, as all her jewellery had been stolen from her room at The George Hotel, and in addition she suffered a heavy fall from Irish Lace at the Waterloo Rails.

For a time it seemed as though there would be a real fight for the team honours between the Russians and the Irish, but when Irish Lace (with the best dressage score of the Irish team) fell, and the final Russian horse Khirurg went clear, the Irish challenge faded.

None of the French horses completed the course without jumping penalties. Garden had one refusal at the fourth fence, the Bullfinch, but with a good time was lying 7th. Just behind was his compatriot André Le Goupil on Jacasse B, also with 20 penalties. The other two French horses both got into difficulties.

So at the end of the day the Russians had a lead of 125·5 points over the Irish; the British were 3rd, another 47 points away; and the French 4th.

The course had done its job admirably: there were seven clear rounds out of 27 starters; only four horses were eliminated; and one retired. All four teams finished. The Waterloo Rails caused the most grief, including the only casualty of the day—Jeremy Smith-Bingham, who was taken to hospital when By Golly fell on him. Otherwise the penalties were well spread around the course. As Mr Sarasin put it: 'The cross-country course, designed and built by a master hand, met all the requirements. Without attaining the severity of an Olympic course, with no traps, but absolutely fair, it nevertheless sorted out the competitors.'

On the final day the Russians looked to be in a secure position, but an exciting finale was in the offing, for the scores of the leading horses were very close.

Harry Freeman-Jackson on St Finbarr, lying 6th, was the first to jump of those that mattered. With a clear round he set the riders ahead of him on edge, and in the end moved up to 4th. Granj also went clear to pose a threat to the leaders, but two other members of the Russian team, Satrap and Khirurg, had thirty penalties each and moved down to 5th and 7th respectively. In spite of the 60 penalties, the gap between the Russians and the Irish remained unbreachable, for Sam Weller also hit two fences and Ballyhoo one.

Then Ryebrooks came in. He jumped clear until the last three fences, but hit two of them and so dropped below Granj. Templer then had to jump clear to win the title. Having already beaten the team riders and therefore having nothing to lose in terms of prestige, he remained very cool, and with only a semblance of a mistake at the water he jumped clear, thus becoming the individual European Champion. Granj was second and Ryebrooks third. The Russians won the team title and the Irish were runners-up.

The Event was judged to have been an unqualified success and the crowd over the three days was estimated at around 22,000. Mr Sarasin reported: 'I do not exaggerate when I say that the impeccable organisation of Three-Day Events has become a truly English speciality. All was carried out without fuss or crisis, with calm and efficiency, everyone knowing his job and appearing to take pleasure in doing it. I can only congratulate the organisers on their work.'

1963

In 1963 Burghley was a standard Three-Day Event, but the international flavour of the previous year was not completely lost. There were three Frenchmen in the list of competitors, and five horses came over from Ireland. One of the French riders was Jacques Le Goff who later became the trainer of the American Three-Day Event team, and to whom much of the credit for their subsequent successes is due.

The dressage test was an elementary one. Performed in a 40-metre arena it was considerably simpler than the FEI test set the previous year, and contained no collected work and no sideways movements. At the end of the dressage, Lieutenant de Croutte, who in 1962 had been in the French team (riding another horse) was in the lead on Microbe. Lars Sederholm, who came originally from Sweden and who has also since become a highly respected trainer, was 6 points behind, riding Char's Choice.

Lochinvar, at the age of six, was making his début at Burghley, ridden not by his owner, Major Derek Allhusen, who had pulled a muscle a few days before, but by Shelagh Kesler. In the dressage they performed a creditable test to share 3rd place with Jacques Le Goff on Laurier. Captain Harry Freeman-Jackson from Ireland—at the age of 52 one of the veterans of the competition—and his great old stager St Finbarr were lying 5th, 7 points behind the leader.

The cross-country course followed more or less the same track as the previous year but was 500 yards shorter. Most of the fences were also the same, though many had been lowered, and there was a new combination at the Maltings which aroused some misgivings in the competitors when they first saw it. The going was perfect.

First off was Richard Meade on Barberry, the only member of the team which had recently won the international Three-Day Event at Munich (where James Templer and M'Lord Connolly had again swept the board) to compete also at Burghley. Barberry at the age of eight was making his first appearance here. The fastest horse across country that Meade has ever ridden, he scored maximum bonus points on both the steeplechase and the cross-country. Handicapped by a poor performance in the dressage, however, he could go no higher than 8th at the end of the day.

Lochinvar and Laurier also scored maximum bonuses, and since they

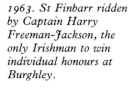

1963. St Finbarr ridden by Captain Harry Freeman-Jackson, the only Irishman to win individual honours at Burghley.

had the same score after the dressage they were again equal after the second day. But in those days the ruling was that in the case of a tie the competitor with the fastest time on the cross-country took precedence, so Lochinvar with a faster round on the cross-country was in the lead. (The rule was subsequently changed to give the competitor with the time nearest to the optimum time the advantage; in 1963 it would have produced the opposite result.) When Microbe had a refusal at the Bull Pens and Char's Choice did not go quite fast enough on the cross-country, dropping to 5th place, nobody could head Lochinvar and Laurier.

Less than a point behind was St Finbarr who also scored the full quota of bonus points. Lying 4th, also having achieved maximum bonus, was Young Pretender, ridden by Michael Bullen—as his former jockey, Frank Weldon, had felt that the time had come to hand over to a younger rider.

Many competitors put up good times. There were no less than nine with maximum bonus on both steeplechase and cross-country, and there was a high percentage of clear rounds. Out of thirty-three starters, sixteen incurred no jumping penalties—which meant that the dressage scores had a greater influence than usual, precluding the possibility of redeeming a poor dressage score with a good time on the cross-country.

On the final day, five horses failed to pass the stiff veterinary inspection, among them Young Pretender. Twenty-one horses were still left in the competition.

The leaders' scores were extremely close and the crowd was already excited when the first of them, Lochinvar, came in. Observers had been impressed with the way Lochinvar, a very good-looking horse, had tackled the cross-country, and it seemed that Major Allhusen had found a worthy successor to his brilliant little mare, Laurien, who had done so well in the fifties. Unfortunately, show jumping was not Lochinvar's strongest suit. He scraped a number of poles—but all stayed in place until the final double, where he hit the rail on the first element. A clear round from Le Goff and Laurier would have made them the outright winners, but they also lowered a fence and therefore remained below Lochinvar and Shelagh Kesler.

St Finbarr and Harry Freeman-Jackson followed: the crowd fully aware that if they could manage a clear round *they* would win. The Master of the Duhallow Hounds was no stranger to pressure—he had first ridden at Badminton in 1950 and had represented Ireland in the Olympics on no less than three occasions. Jumping in a style that might have been more familiar in the hunting field than in a jumping arena, St Finbarr made no semblance of a mistake and was greeted with a roar from the crowd, of a volume reserved only for real heroes. So for the first time at Burghley the green coat of the Irish was seen at the head of the winners' parade. Lochinvar and Shelagh Kesler were 2nd and Jacques Le Goff with Laurier 3rd.

1964

In 1964 Burghley was to be the last public outing for the horses and riders who were to represent Britain at the Tokyo Olympics five weeks later. The team, to be announced after Burghley, was to be chosen from a short-list of six riders and seven horses.

Two of the short-listed horses, Young Pretender and By Golly, were lame and did not compete. Captain James Templer and M'Lord Connolly—winners of Badminton—and Michael Bullen and Sea Breeze, who had sufficiently convincing claims to be included in the team, completed only part of the competition. The rest of the short-listed horses and riders were expected to go all out to prove their worth for the two remaining team places. The competition was intense, with thirty-five riders—including four from Germany and two from Ireland—presenting themselves before the dressage judges.

Sheila Waddington, who as Sheila Willcox had been the most successful horse trials rider of the late fifties, had retired in 1959, but when the rules were changed to allow women to ride in the Olympic Three-Day Event she decided to make a bid for the team. With this in view she had bought Glenamoy the previous year. Having won the Little Badminton event in the spring—the horse's first Three-Day Event—they were included in the Selectors' short list. At Burghley Sheila Waddington displayed all her old mastery in the dressage, performing an accurate, precise test for 37·5 penalties, which took her into equal first place.

Sharing the lead was one of the German horses, King, ridden by Ludwig Goessing. His compatriot, Jochem Mehrdorf on Iltschi, was 3rd. None of the German horses appearing at Burghley was short-listed for the Olympics but these two had competed *hors concours* at Badminton in the spring because they were not fully fit. Then followed the rest of the potential Olympic combinations—Master Bernard and Staff-Sergeant Ben Jones (4th), James Templer and M'Lord Connolly (5th), Jeremy Beale and Victoria Bridge (7th) and Michael Bullen and Sea Breeze (8th). Only Richard Meade on Barberry could breach their ranks: with a good test for 45·5 penalties they were lying 6th. Having fallen in the lake at Badminton they had not been included in the short list, but at the Eridge Two-Day Event three weeks before, they had trounced all the Selectors' favourites and were out to do so again.

The cross-country course was judged to be relatively straightforward by the competitors when they walked it, though the Trout Hatchery—approached down the hill with a log in and a post and rails of 3 ft. 4 in. out—and the drop fence on the brink of Capability's Cutting were thought likely to cause trouble. The steeplechase course had been moved to a new site just south of the lake, which was convenient for the spectators but difficult to ride because of the undulations.

On cross-country day the weather was perfect, but the hot summer that had brought the earliest harvest for many years had dried out the ground and the going was firm.

M'Lord Connolly, first to go, jumped only the first nine fences as instructed, in copy book style. But Victoria Bridge retired lame after the first fence and was later found to have slipped his stifle.

The compulsory 10-minute halt between the second roads and tracks and the cross-country was introduced for the first time and resulted in some competitors making errors in their timing of Phase C. Ben Jones on Master Bernard was one of them, and incurred an expensive 18 penalties, so in spite of a maximum bonus on the steeplechase and a fast clear round on the cross-country, he lost the lead and ended the day in 2nd place.

Four horses gained maximum bonus on the cross-country. Marshall Tudor and William Leigh incurred 20 penalties in the process but Lochinvar ridden by Derek Allhusen, Durlas Eile ridden by Eddie Boylan from Ireland, and Barberry, all jumped clear. Lochinvar and Barberry had also gained maximum points on the steeplechase, and Barberry's score was

*1964. Richard Meade
and Barberry at the
Trout Hatchery on their
way to achieving
maximum bonus.*

good enough to put him in the lead. Lochinvar went into 4th place and Durlas Eile, only recently bought by Eddie Boylan, was 5th.

Iltschi had dropped a few marks on the steeplechase but with a fast cross-country round was lying 3rd at the end of the day. King and Goessing went faster but had one refusal.

Kilmacthomas and Mary Macdonell, runners-up in the 1963 Pony Club Championships, proved that they had successfully made the transition to adult horse trials with a good clear round which put them into 7th place.

Sheila Waddington and Glenamoy were almost last to go. Glenamoy had too much knee action to be a really fast horse, and in order to improve her chances of doing a good time Sheila Waddington had given him a stimulant (this was before such drugs were banned). He completed the steeplechase within the optimum time but afterwards was completely exhausted, and Sheila had to nurse a very tired horse round the cross-country. Her hopes of a place in the Olympic team were dashed when he refused at Capability's Cutting and took a ducking in the Trout Hatchery.

On the final day Durlas Eile was the first of the leaders to jump. He incurred 10 penalties but still managed to move up to 4th place. Following him, Lochinvar refused at the water, tipping off Derek Allhusen who notched no less than 90·5 penalties, thus dropping ten places to finish 14th. When Master Bernard had one fence down he changed places with Iltschi who moved up to 2nd with a clear round. Richard Meade could afford to knock one fence down but rounded off a very fine performance with a good clear round. It was Meade's first win in a major Three-Day Event and he was particularly pleased to beat all the Olympic hopefuls.

Note The Selectors, impressed with Barberry's performance at Burghley, included him in the Olympic team, and it was felt that Ben Jones and Master Bernard had fully earned the fourth place. In Tokyo the two senior team members, James Templer and Michael Bullen were both eliminated, while Barberry and Master Bernard both went clear in the cross-country. At the end of the speed and endurance Master Bernard was lying 5th and Barberry was in the lead—only to drop to 8th with three fences down in the jumping. Master Bernard also had three fences down and finished 9th.

In spite of the fact that the five top horses were in Moscow contesting the European Championships, there were some high class competitors in the field of thirty-four. Five riders came over from Ireland—among them Alan Lillingston, a former steeplechase jockey and one of very few amateurs to win the Champion Hurdle.

1965 was memorable for the appalling weather conditions in which the dressage took place. Newspaper reporters, unfamiliar with the stoicism with which riders have to treat all kinds of weather, were impressed that they seemed undaunted and managed to be immaculately turned out.

One of the pre-competition favourites, Corporal of the Horse Alan Doxey, riding Sea Breeze (a team horse in the 1964 Olympics, then ridden by Michael Bullen) led the dressage with a score of 59·5. Only 2·4 points behind was Captain Jeremy Beale on Victoria Bridge, who had been injured on the cross-country the previous year at Burghley. None of the other competitors could produce dressage tests of the same standard as the two leaders. Twelve points behind in 3rd place was Rosemary Kopanski on The Little Mermaid who had been 3rd in the Little Badminton event in the spring.

The weather improved for cross-country day and the ground dried out remarkably quickly. But there were not to be many fast times either on the steeplechase, set once again across the lake in front of the house, or on the cross-country course, which was not much altered from the year before.

Victoria Bridge went extremely well, only just missing maximum bonus on the steeplechase, and then clocked the fastest time of the day on the cross-country. This put him in a commanding lead, which was increased considerably when Sea Breeze refused twice and then fell at the Sunken Wall. Rise and Shine, ridden by Marietta Speed (now Fox-Pitt) who had finished 4th at Badminton and had been in training for the Moscow team, was one of only two horses to gain maximum bonus on the steeplechase and was only slightly slower than Victoria Bridge on the cross-country. Rise and Shine had been 30 points behind Victoria Bridge in the dressage and the margin was slightly widened after the cross-country, but nobody could get any closer.

Lying 3rd at the end of the day was Priam, ridden by Jennifer Graham-Clark, who was also in 5th place with her other horse French Frolic. The

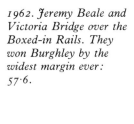

1962. Jeremy Beale and Victoria Bridge over the Boxed-in Rails. They won Burghley by the widest margin ever: 57·6.

wo were separated by Charm, ridden by Prudence Cawston. Anne Lewis-
Smith, a columnist in the *Stamford Mercury*, wrote of the lady riders:
'Miss Graham-Clark wore a black crash helmet with her fair hair sticking
out from under it for the steeplechasing and, following her, Lady Hugh
Russell (who rode Turnstone but had a fall on the cross-country) was most
elegant in a light navy jockey cap and sweater with cream jodhpurs. I must
say all the women riders were amazingly neat. Even after a fall all the
disarray I could spot in one rider was on her shoulders; not a hair had
escaped from her neat net. I feel many watchers with their hair blown by
the wind and mud-splashed stockings must have envied their ability to
remain so unruffled!'

None of the Irish contingent escaped cross-country penalties—Alan
Lillingston incurring 60. The Poacher and Martin Whiteley, who earlier in
the year had won the Little Badminton Event, had two refusals, and The
Little Mermaid did a slow clear to finish in 7th place.

As far as the show jumping was concerned, Victoria Bridge was in an
unassailable position—barring disasters—but there was much jostling in
the lower placings. Jennifer Graham-Clark's horses each had 20 penalties:
French Frolic slipping to 7th place and Priam to 4th. Charm also hit two
fences and dropped to 6th.

Pollyann Hely-Hutchinson (now Lochore) on Count Jasper, who had
gone well round the cross-country without putting up a spectacular time,
had 10 penalties in the show jumping but moved up from 6th to 5th. Merry
Judge and Jane Walkington completed one of only five clear rounds and
made a dramatic climb in the order from 8th after the cross-country to 3rd.
Rise and Shine hit two fences but had accumulated sufficient advantage the
previous day to avoid being displaced. Victoria Bridge rounded off an
extremely good performance with a neat clear round to win by a margin of
57·6 points—the highest in the history of Burghley.

So Jeremy Beale went home with the Bass Challenge trophy for the
winning rider, a cheque for £250 and the prospect of a new pair of
breeches which are traditionally awarded to the winning rider by Bernard
Weatherill Ltd.

1966
WORLD CHAMPIONSHIPS

In the early 1960s the FEI decided to institute World Championships for
horse trials, to take place at four-yearly intervals half way through the
Olympic cycle. England was invited to stage the first competition, to be
held in 1966, and so it came to Burghley.

The World Championships got off to a chequered start when restrictions
imposed by the Ministry of Agriculture because of an outbreak of swamp
fever on the Continent meant that none of the Western European nations
could compete. Nevertheless the competition had a fairly global aspect for
there were teams from Argentina—whose horses spent a month in quarantine at the RAVC depot at Melton Mowbray—the USA, the USSR and
Ireland. The Irish had kept everybody on tenterhooks as to whether or
not they would be coming, and it was only at the last minute that their
Ministry of Agriculture allowed them to compete.

Though there were not many teams, those that came had some good
form behind them. Among the Argentinians was the silver medallist of the
1964 Tokyo Olympics, Chalan ridden by Carlos Moratorio. The Russians
had won the European Championships at Burghley in 1962, and were

fielding two of their winning horses. In the team was Rumb, ridden by Boris Konjkov, and competing as an individual was Khirurg, now ridden by Valery Suvorov, who had been 7th in 1962 when ridden by Lev Baklyshkin. Guerman Gazjumov who had finished 2nd in 1962 and 10th in the Olympics on Granj was riding Gret. In Tokyo the Russian team had been 5th.

The American team had won the silver medal in Tokyo and their team for Burghley included one of the Tokyo horses, Gallopade, now ridden by Rick Eckhardt (in Tokyo he had been ridden by Kevin Freeman), and two riders from that team—Freeman and Michael Plumb. At Burghley, Freeman was riding M'Lord Connolly on whom James Templer had won the 1962 European Championships. The Irish had Eddie Boylan on Durlas Eile, winners at Badminton the year before, as their strongest card.

As far as the British team was concerned the task of the Selectors had been made more difficult by the cancellation of Badminton in the spring. They did not announce the team until the last minute—which was fortunate, as at the vets' inspection Mary Macdonell's Kilmacthomas, who would almost certainly have been included in the team, was found to be lame. So the chosen four were Annette Ling and The Lavender Cowboy, winners over a stiff course at the Punchestown Three-Day Event three weeks before; Marietta Speed and Rise and Shine, runners-up in the same competition, as well as at Burghley in 1965; Christine Sheppard and Fenjirao, winner of the recent Eridge Two-Day Event; and Richard Meade and Barberry.

The field was made up to a total of thirty-nine by thirteen British individuals, for whom the qualifications were slightly stiffer than for a normal year.

The competition took place in beautiful weather. The Queen, Prince Philip and Princess Margaret were all staying at Burghley, and a record crowd for those days, estimated at 27,000, came to watch.

After the dressage the Russians were in the lead: counting the best three scores they had a total of 144. The Argentinians were 2nd, only 9 points behind; the Irish 3rd; the British 4th; and the Americans 5th. Chalan performed the best test for 42.5 penalties, but he had only a small margin over the Russian horse Gret, ridden by Guerman Gazjumov. The Russians and the Argentinians between them monopolised the top places and only Eddie Boylan and Durlas Eile in 6th and Fenjirao in 8th place, made any impression on them. None of the Americans was in the top ten.

The multiplying factor was set at 1.5 which meant that the technical delegate considered the cross-country course to be difficult. Bill Thomson had built a highly imaginative course of genuine World Championship standard. Richard Meade, whose experience includes three Olympics and international championships in many parts of the world as well as many Badmintons, considers it to be the biggest course he has ever ridden. And in the opinion of Martin Whiteley it was not only the biggest course he had ever ridden but the best of all the championship courses he has seen.

The course was the same length as it had been in 1962. The steeplechase, situated for the first time on the golf course, was 2 miles 416 yards, the cross-country was $4\frac{3}{4}$ miles and the total distance was $18\frac{1}{2}$ miles. The cross-country course went in the same direction as it does now but finished with a loop towards the road between Stamford and the stables, a part of the park included only once since, in 1973. The statistics make it an average year for

there were ten clear rounds, and fourteen horses failed to finish; but the twenty-three falls were considerably more than usual.

The fence that caused the most trouble was the Coffin, situated towards the end of the course. Six horses fell there—in most cases because they were going too fast—and four others refused. The Footbridge, a big fence —3 ft. 9 in. with a spread of 6 ft. 7 in.—with an awkward approach, also caused trouble.

One of Bill Thomson's most ingenious creations ever was the Spray Fence which consisted of a square-cut silver-painted rail from which jets of water poured into a wide ditch. The prospect of the system breaking down—the water was pumped from the lake—was something of a nightmare to the course builder, and at the time the fence was denounced as a gimmick.

The mechanism worked perfectly and most horses flew it—but the first to go, Lochinvar, ridden by Derek Allhusen, stopped suddenly and deposited his rider in the ditch. It was also responsible for eliminating

1966, the World Championships. (Above) Individual Champions Carlos Moratorio and Chalan from Argentina clear the Footbridge. (Below) Team Champions, Ireland: (left to right) Eddie Boylan and Durlas Eile (4th), Virginia Freeman-Jackson and Sam Weller (3rd), Penny Moreton and Loughlin (8th), Tommy Brennan and Kilkenny (14th). With them is Captain Harry Freeman-Jackson.

Marietta Speed, as Rise and Shine would go nowhere near it. It was perhaps because of the effect that it had on Rise and Shine that people were critical of the fence, for as The Lavender Cowboy had earlier been eliminated at the Dairy Farm it put the British team out of the competition.

However, the other two team horses both went very well. Fenjirao went clear earning a bonus of 53·2 (maximum was 86) and ending the day in 6th place. Barberry, last of the team to go, achieved an outstanding round— according to his rider it was his finest hour—and was one of only three horses to score maximum bonus. After the dressage he had been lying 20th—what started as a good test having been spoiled when Barberry was upset by crackles from the loudspeaker. By the end of the cross-country he had moved up to 4th.

The Irish horse Sam Weller, ridden by Virginia Freeman-Jackson (who a few days after Burghley married Lord Petersham) also gained maximum bonus on the cross-country, as did Rondman ridden by Captain A. D. Brooks, though he had a fall at the Coffin in the process. An outstanding cross-country rider, Virginia Freeman-Jackson lost her hat at the sixth fence but rode her 15·1½ hh veteran with great dash, hair flying, and did well to stay on when Sam Weller very nearly fell at the Coffin. At the end of the day she was lying 2nd, just over 10 points ahead of her team mate, Eddie Boylan, first of the Irish to go, who rode a captain's round, taking no chances, for a bonus of 67·6. Ireland was the only team with all four members round—Penny Moreton on Loughlin went clear, but Kilkenny ridden by Tommy Brennan (6th in Mexico when ridden by the American Jimmy Wofford) had a fall at the Footbridge.

Of the Russian horses, Rumb and Boris Konjkov were lying 7th at the end of the day, and Pavel Deev on Paket was 8th, each having had one refusal. Two years later Paket was to show that his form at Burghley was no fluke, for in the Mexico Olympics he was in the lead after the cross-country, only to be eliminated when his rider went the wrong way in the show jumping. Gret also completed the course with one refusal—at the Trout Hatchery—but had recorded a slow time on the steeplechase; and the fourth Russian horse, Rulon, retired towards the end of an eventful round.

One member of the Argentinian team retired and two completed the course with 40 jumping penalties each. Chalan redeemed the day for Argentina with a superb round. Moratorio, who was described by Colonel Frank Weldon in *L'Année Hippique* as 'a thoughtful, intelligent, painstaking rider rather than dashing or brilliant', made no mistakes and returned a very good bonus of 78, which left him comfortably ahead of Sam Weller.

The American team was eliminated, as Foster and Michael Plumb had three refusals at the Trout Hatchery, and Bean Platter and Brad Smith retired after two falls. Kevin Freeman and M'Lord Connolly had a fall at the Footbridge but they were the only ones among the six American entries to complete the competition, as Gallopade, who also fell, was withdrawn before the show jumping. Michael Plumb riding his second horse, Chakola, was again eliminated—this time at the Spray Fence, and Kevin Freeman on his other horse, Royal Imp, retired.

The Poacher, ridden by Martin Whiteley, was the only individual to outshine the team members. It was the best ride that The Poacher ever gave Whiteley; on the brink of running away, he was foot perfect at the fences and clocked a fast time for 64 bonus points. They finished the day in

5th place and set those who are that way inclined muttering about the 'lack of perspicacity' of the Selectors. If The Poacher, at that time aged ten and winner of the Little Badminton Event the previous year, had been in the team the British would have been in the lead. But according to his rider, who was on the Selection Committee, there was no question of The Poacher being in the team, for he had not put up a very good performance at Burghley the year before and there had been no Badminton to redeem it.

Dreamy Dasher ridden by Tom Durston-Smith also went extremely well on the cross-country. So did Rosemary Kopanski on Plain Sailing and Susan Cavenagh on Landsman, although they were both considerably slower than Dreamy Dasher.

After the speed and endurance the Irish with plus 110 had a lead of 92 points over the Russians. The Argentinian team was originally eliminated as Ludovico Fugco failed to weigh-in after the cross-country, but since he clearly made the weight without the help of his saddle a merciful jury reinstated him. So the team was 3rd with minus 173·8.

On the final day the best Russian horse, Rumb, was clearly lame and was spun by the inspection panel—in spite of strenuous protests. So the Russians, having already had another horse retired on the cross-country, joined the ranks of the eliminated.

As far as the teams were concerned, the show jumping was almost a formality, for the Irish had 283 points in hand. They duly won and the Argentinians were 2nd.

In the individual contest the scores were very close and there was a tense and exciting climax to the competition. Durlas Eile, lying 3rd, was the first of the leaders to go, and when he had a fence down his score put him below Barberry. Then Sam Weller lying 2nd came in. His supporters were on edge, for in the European Championship in 1962 he had knocked two fences down. In 1966 he repeated the performance, and with 20 penalties he, too, dropped below Barberry. Moratorio knew that he could have two fences down and still win—but he hit only one and so was assured of the title. Barberry was still to go and if he could manage a clear he would move up to second place. There were vivid memories of Tokyo, when they had been in the lead after the cross-country but had dropped to 8th with three fences down in the jumping. But on this occasion there were no disasters and Barberry jumped a confident clear round to take the offered 2nd place. The Poacher also jumped clear but stayed in 5th place.

So though it was hardly a fully representative World Championships the performance of the Irish with three good scores and all four members completing would have stood them in good stead whatever the opposition. And Chalan and Moratorio who had led all the way through the competition had fully earned their Gold Medal.

1967

'The 1000-to-1 Skewbald Wins Burghley'. 'Popadom surprises the Pundits'. 'Burghley—A Story Book Result'. So ran the headlines after Lorna Sutherland's victory on her hog-maned skewbald cob. It was a remarkable achievement, for Lorna, at the age of twenty-three, was riding in only her third Three-Day Event—Badminton in the spring had been the first—and Popadom was a totally unconsidered outsider. Also, the opposition was stiff. Among those competing were Major Allhusen on Lochinvar, who had been in the winning team and 3rd individually in the

1967. Lorna Sutherland and Popadom at Fence 6, the Open Ditch.

European Championships at Punchestown a month earlier; and the previous year's champion, Chalan, who had been bought by the American rider Bill Haggard for a figure reputed to be in the region of £10,000—a huge sum for those days. There was a strong Irish contingent, and an exotic note was given to the competition by three riders from Japan. In an attempt to put the sport on the map in their country the Japanese had purchased a number of European horses and had also competed at Punchestown.

Popadom, whose sire was thoroughbred but whose dam had spent most of her career pulling a cart, had disgraced his rider in the dressage at Stokenchurch the week before. Since then he had been subjected to merciless drilling and had hardly been allowed off the bit. At Burghley, three hours' work before the dressage paid dividends, for in the arena he was completely obedient, straight and light on his feet. In spite of the fact that he was incapable of showing extension he was well rewarded and earned the very good score of 28 penalties. This put him comfortably in the lead and there were only two others below the 50 mark—Staff-Sergeant Ben Jones on Apollo (37) and Juliet Jobling-Purser from Ireland on Jenny (48.33).

Chalan was lying 4th with 50 penalties, and Lochinvar 5th. Althea Roger Smith on her six-year-old grey, Questionnaire, who had gained a resounding victory at Kinlet earlier in the year, was 6th. In 7th place was Lorna Sutherland on her other horse, Nicholas Nickleby, who was both better bred and better known than his stablemate.

The cross-country course was a scaled-down version of that used for the World Championships, but it included no fewer than six fences with ditches on the take-off side, and was still a demanding course. Forty-five horses started the speed and endurance test; one retired on the steeplechase and three were considered unfit to continue by the veterinary panel at the end of Phase C. On the cross-country there were twenty-three clear rounds (an unusually high number), three horses were eliminated, and five retired.

Three horses—Questionnaire, Rock On, ridden by Mark Phillips, and Evening Mail ridden by an American girl, Sara Lord—gained maximum bonus on the cross-country (75·6). Lorna Sutherland, after a fast round on Nicholas Nickleby, which put her into 3rd place at the end of the day, was determined to cock a snook at all those who had said that Popadom would not be fast enough to maintain his advantage. She had to show him the whip on the steeplechase in order to persuade him to keep up the gallop for maximum bonus. However, by the time she set off on the cross-country, she knew that her nearest rival, Apollo, had been eliminated at the Trout Hatchery, and so she had a certain amount of leeway. She returned with a bonus of 61·2, one of the fastest times and good enough to maintain the lead, 10 points ahead of Questionnaire.

Lochinvar had also gone well and was lying 4th, and Chalan was 5th. A rather slow time on the cross-country put the Irish horse Jenny out of the hunt. Of the Japanese riders, one was eliminated, one had 140 jumping penalties and Mikio Shiba on Josephine (who had been bought from Major Eddie Boylan) went clear but was also handicapped by a slow time.

On the final day the marks were extremely close. At that time the jumping was carried out in numerical order, but since the leader was last to go an exciting finish was guaranteed. The drama began almost immediately, for Nicholas Nickleby, lying 3rd, was second into the ring. He was jumping well, when suddenly the bell rang. Lorna thought it had nothing to do with her, and finished the course without hitting any of the fences. But she had missed out the ninth fence and so was summarily eliminated.

Further upsets occurred when Lochinvar and Chalan each had 20 penalties and so slipped to 5th and 7th respectively. Rock On, and Our Nobby ridden by Jane Bullen, who had a fast round on the cross-country but could not manage the maximum bonus on the steeplechase, both jumped clear and moved up five places—Rock On to 4th and Our Nobby to 3rd.

Althea Roger Smith, who was better known as a show jumping rider and who had already qualified Questionnaire for the final of the Foxhunter show jumping competition at the Horse of the Year Show, still had to use all her skill to coax a clear round from her horse. In doing so she raised the hopes of the Ovaltine seller (in those days free Ovaltine was available to competitors) who was rumoured to have wagered £50 on her winning. But Popadom, who could afford one fence down, bounced round without the semblance of a mistake and delighted the enthusiastic crowd with a series of circus bucks on the lap of honour.

1968

In 1968 great additional interest was given to the competition with the appearance of ten horses and seven riders short-listed for the team to compete in the Mexico Olympics. Their form at Burghley was to help the Selectors make their final choice.

In the dressage, however, the top English riders had to yield to a young American, Mason Phelps, riding Argonaut, who performed a beautiful test for only 34 penalties. Richard Meade on Barberry also gave a very high-class performance in the arena to come 2nd with 37·67. Barberry, at the age of thirteen, had an outstanding career behind him; in addition to two brilliant performances at Burghley in 1964 and 1966 he had been 8th in the Tokyo Olympics. He was virtually certain of a place in the team and had been excused Badminton in the spring.

Third after the dressage was Fair and Square ridden by Sheila Willcox, winner of Badminton on three consecutive occasions in the late fifties, but not at this point on the Olympic short list. The Lavender Cowboy, ridden by Mark Phillips, whose other horse Rock On was lame, shared 4th place with the only Frenchman in the field, Henri Michel, riding Ouragan C.

Of the other selected horses, Lochinvar, ridden by Major Derek Allhusen, went well for 53·67 penalties and 6th place, but The Poacher ridden by Martin Whiteley was off form and was only 21st. Staff-Sergeant Ben Jones, riding two horses with the same name, was 18th on Brigadier Gordon-Watson's great Cornishman V and 7th on Bridget Parker's Cornishman. Last of the short-listed horses, in 33rd place, was Our Nobby ridden by Jane Bullen. Thirteen years old and only 15 hands, Our Nobby had won Badminton in the spring. Since then considerable work had been put into improving his dressage, but at Burghley he showed his distaste for this phase and at one moment almost jumped out of the arena.

The cross-country course was considerably changed from the previous year. It was felt that the trickiest fences would be the Trout Hatchery—with a log both in and out—Fence 23, a post and rails at the foot of a bank with a ditch on the landing side, and the following fence which replaced the Footbridge in the ditch below the arena. This was a tricky combination which offered the possibility of saving time by jumping a corner.

Cross-country day was fine but the air was humid and the going—unusually for Burghley—was holding, as a result of recent rain. The first of the short-listed horses to go, The Lavender Cowboy, was eliminated at Fence 24. Cornishman V refused at the Trout Hatchery, but Our Nobby restored the Selectors' confidence with a brilliant round in the third fastest time. This left him in 5th place at the end of the day. Proving that lack of size is no disadvantage, Sue Neill's Peri, a Grade A show jumper but also only 15 hands, went even faster than Our Nobby to move up to 3rd place.

Then Lochinvar and his 54-year-old rider gave the Selectors another boost with a very good round in a fast time, finishing with a score that nobody could better. Ouragan C also went well to keep the 4th place he had occupied after the dressage. Following him Sheila Willcox and Fair and Square clocked almost the same time, but by dint of a better dressage score they went into 2nd place. Sheila considers Fair and Square, the sire of Be Fair, to be the best horse she has ever had. He was small but fast and athletic, and exceptionally intelligent.

Martin Whiteley, who was suffering from a back injury, found The Poacher strong, had difficulty turning into the 24th fence, and incurred two refusals. Argonaut was retired after giving his rider no less than three falls. He had an unusual number of falls in his career and it seemed as though he suffered some kind of mental black-out at the last moment before take off. Ben Jones again had one refusal on his second Cornishman.

Right at the end of the day a dampener was cast on the atmosphere when Barberry, with a good chance of taking the lead, fell at the 23rd fence where the bank was slippery, and injured his back. The extent of the damage was not immediately known, but it later became clear that he would not recover in time for Mexico.

The course had proved difficult. Out of forty-one horses who started Phase A, only eight went clear, and nineteen failed to finish.

After the cross-country, Lochinvar and Fair and Square, lying 1st and

2nd, were both lame. Throughout the night Fair and Square's connections worked on him, and he trotted sound before the inspection panel in the morning. Lochinvar also passed the inspection, but with Mexico in mind, Derek Allhusen felt that it would be unwise to take any risks, and on veterinary advice withdrew him.

So Sheila Willcox was left in the lead. In the show jumping, when Peri—who had moved up to 2nd as a result of Lochinvar's withdrawal—had 10 penalties, Fair and Square could afford to hit one fence without losing his position. He jumped well, made no mistakes, and incurred only 0.5 of a time fault. Thus the Burghley title was added to the many others that Sheila Willcox had already won. Our Nobby jumped clear and moved up to 3rd, above Ouragan C, who retreated once more to his 4th position.

Note After Burghley the Selectors announced that Our Nobby and Lochinvar were to be included in the team, and so was Richard Meade. He was to ride Lady Hugh Russell's Turnstone, who had been withdrawn after the dressage at Burghley but on whom Meade had finished 2nd at Badminton. The fourth place would be filled either by Sheila Willcox or by some combination of Ben Jones or Mark Phillips on one of the two Cornishmen, or on The Poacher, who Martin Whiteley had put at the disposal of the Selection Committee. As it happened, Turnstone went lame, so Richard Meade found a new partner in Cornishman V, and Ben Jones quickly established a rapport with The Poacher.

Sheila Willcox declined the invitation to go to Mexico as reserve. Shaitan who, ridden by Gillian Watson, had gone well at Burghley to finish 6th, went as the reserve horse and Mark Phillips was named as reserve rider. Paradoxically the somewhat fraught selection process brought positive results, for the team came back in triumph with the Gold Medal; Major Allhusen and Lochinvar won the individual Silver; Cornishman was 4th and The Poacher 5th.

1968. Sheila Willcox and Fair and Square make light work of Fence 23, rails and ditch, which caused so much trouble.

1969

In 1969 Burghley was again used as a final work-out for the horses who were to represent Britain in an international. This time it was to be in the European Championships at Haras-du-Pin in France, to be held in two weeks' time. The six horses selected were named on the first day of the trials and they competed *hors concours*: they were excused the steeplechase and were only to jump half the cross-country fences. It turned out to be a classic example of the wisdom of the old adage 'bad dress rehearsal good performance', for the selected horses did not on the whole distinguish themselves at their warm-up and the headline in the *Daily Telegraph* afterwards was 'British Team does not Impress'.

Three of the short-listed combinations led the dressage: The Poacher, ridden by Staff-Sergeant Ben Jones of the RHA, showed what a high class dressage horse he was by performing easily the best test for 35·67 penalties; and Richard Walker on Pasha, winners at Badminton in the spring and holders of the European Junior Championship title, also went well to come 2nd, 11 points behind The Poacher. Among the team 'definites', Major Allhusen on Lochinvar, individual silver medallists in Mexico, were lying 3rd with a score of 53.

Just behind with 53·33 penalty points were Lorna Sutherland and her skewbald, Popadom, winners at Burghley in 1967. They performed their usual accurate and precise test to head the list of those who were competing fully in the Three-Day Event. Lorna Sutherland was also lying 2nd on her other skewbald, Gypsy Flame. They had a slightly better score than the remaining short-listed horses—Pollyann Hely-Hutchinson on Count Jasper, Celia Ross-Taylor on Jonathan, and Mary Gordon-Watson on Cornishman V, who all had scores in the upper 50s.

Gillian Watson and Shaitan, an eight-year-old part-bred Arab who had gone to Mexico as reserve horse, were lying 3rd after the dressage, and Angela Sowden (now Tucker) was 4th on Mooncoin.

Of the thirty-two horses in the competition, seven failed to complete the cross-country course and seven jumped clear. There were a number of tricky fences which posed problems even to the experienced team horses, but although there were few clear rounds, the course caused considerably less grief than the year before.

Both The Poacher and Pasha came unstuck on the cross-country. The Poacher fell at the Waterloo Rails. Pasha, having been excused the steeplechase, was difficult to control without the long gallop to settle him. He went too fast at Fence 24 and came down. Undaunted, his nineteen-year-old rider put him at the awkward corner at the Bass Charrington rails, but he ran out, and did so again when faced at another corner at Fence 27, the 'Z' fence. Cornishman, who was slightly lame, did not start on the cross-country, but Lochinvar, Jonathan and Count Jasper all did what was asked of them without mistakes.

Popadom jumped clear, but as he had recently been off work with a virus, his rider did not push him; with a bonus of 34·8 he finished the day in 4th place. Gypsy Flame, of more aristocratic lineage than her stablemate, went considerably faster. However, never reliable at corners, she ran out twice when faced at the corner of the 'Z' fence, and so dropped out of the running. Gill Watson and Shaitan went the safest way at the alternative fences, but as this was an exceptionally handy little horse they wasted little time. They returned the fastest time of the day and took over the lead. Skyborn and Michael Tucker, 17th after the dressage, went almost as fast and survived a near disaster when they misjudged the corner at the Bass Charrington rails. By the end of the day they had moved up fifteen places and were lying 2nd, 18·6 points behind Shaitan. Corncrake, ridden by Colonel Mark Darley who had won Badminton seventeen years earlier, moved up to 3rd place after a good cross-country round; and Peri and Sue Neill, 2nd at Burghley in 1968, had one refusal but a good time put them in 5th place.

The show jumping was not of the highest standard: of the team horses Lochinvar had three fences down and The Poacher two. The over-all order changed when Popadom and Peri both jumped clear to move up to 3rd and 4th above Corncrake, who refused at the water. Michael Tucker and Skyborn had one fence down, allowing Gill Watson two fences in hand. In an eventful round Shaitan, who was usually a reliable show jumper, rattled a number of fences, lowered two and so used up their quota and no more. So Gill Watson and Shaitan duly won the £250 1st prize and Michael Tucker and Skyborn took home the £150 for 2nd.

Note At Haras-du-Pin, where Bill Thomson was the technical delegate, the British team horses duly found the form that had eluded them at Burghley. Lochinvar, The Poacher, Count Jasper and Pasha were finally selected for the team. Jonathan had to be left behind as there were doubts about his soundness; and Mary Gordon-Watson on Cornishman and Mark Phillips on Rock On, who had not been at Burghley, competed as individuals.

The team led the dressage—The Poacher again performing the best test, later to be marred by two falls on the cross-country—retained their lead, and in the end won easily from the Russians. A superb performance over the enormous cross-country course gave Mary Gordon-Watson the individual title, and Richard Walker was the runner-up (thus narrowly missing being both Junior and Senior European Champion). The individual win gave Britain the right to stage the next European Championships, and thus they returned to Burghley in 1971.

1969. Gillian Watson and Shaitan jump the Sunken Wall.

1970

In 1970 the leading British riders were not competing at Burghley as they were preparing for the trip to the World Championships at Punchestown. There, the following week they were to win a decisive victory—with Mark Phillips on Chicago, Stewart Stevens on Benson, Richard Meade on The Poacher and Mary Gordon-Watson on Cornishman V carrying off the team title, and the latter also winning the individual championship.

In spite of their absence, Burghley was as colourful and as well supported as ever. Of particular interest were the first appearances of some of the young horses and riders who in the following years were to play an important part in British teams. Baccarat ridden by Debbie West, Larkspur ridden by Janet Hodgson, and Smokey VI, ridden at the time by Bill Powell-Harris from Ireland, were all competing at Burghley for the first time. So was Chris Collins, riding Tawny Port.

In the dressage, Judy Bradwell and Don Camillo took the lead over the thirty-two starters with a very good test which scored 28·67 penalties. Shortly before, Don Camillo, aged 10, had been sold as a hunter by Debbie West who had ridden him in his previous competitions; he had competed at Burghley in 1969 but had trouble on the cross-country. With some months to go before his owner, Mr Ruff Smith, needed him for the Quorn opening meet, it was agreed that Judy Bradwell should ride him at Burghley.

Lying 2nd in the dressage was Off Centre ridden by James Templer, former winner of both Badminton and Burghley, and 3rd (14 points behind the leader) was David Goldie from Troon in Scotland on Rembrandt.

The cross-country was slightly deceptive, for although many of the fences were below maximum height there were a number of tricky combinations which required thought from the riders and very accurate steering. Ten horses failed to finish the course, and there were twelve clear rounds.

Soon after the day began Baccarat showed what an outstanding cross-country horse he was by scoring a maximum bonus on the steeplechase and dropping only three points on Phase D for the second fastest time of the day. A mere 15·1½ hands, he was at the time only seven, but already had a 5th place at Badminton behind him. However, with a moderate dressage score he could move no higher than 5th place at the end of the speed and endurance test.

Course specialist Peri, ridden by Sue Neill who was 2nd in 1968 and 4th in 1969, went almost as well to finish only one place behind. Chris Collins had a crashing fall on the steeplechase and retired—somewhat ironically for a former champion amateur steeplechase jockey. His future partner, Smokey, then aged only six, must have been smarting from the indignity of coming last in the dressage, for he raced round the cross-country to score the only maximum bonus (75·6) of the day. This was the last year that the bonus system of scoring was used. In 1971 it was replaced by an all penalty point system so the phrase 'maximum bonus' associated with so many outstanding performances disappeared from eventing vocabulary.

Don Camillo did not go flat out. He jumped well without taking any of the fences the most difficult way, scoring a bonus of 54·8 which put him in a good but by no means unassailable position. Rembrandt was also faultless at the fences, and his faster time gave him exactly the same score as Don Camillo. Upper Strata, ridden by Richard Walker—who on Pasha had won Badminton the previous year and had been second in the European Championships at Haras-du-Pin—also went fast and clear to finish the day

1970. Judy Bradwell and Don Camillo over the Rails and Ditch.

in 4th place. They were just beaten by Janet Hodgson and Larkspur who went even faster.

James Templer and Off Centre fell at the Bull Pens and retired. The previous year's winners, Gillian Watson and Shaitan, were eliminated at the pen out of Chabonel Spinney. Usually a very genuine horse, Shaitan was later found to be suffering from a bad back.

The show jumping course, set by Denzil Oxby, for some unknown reason caused trouble, and there were only five clear rounds. Baccarat stayed in 5th place in spite of having a fence down, but Larkspur, who also had 10 penalties, dropped one place to 4th. Upper Strata, who had been brought over from Australia as a show jumper, predictably went clear and so moved above Larkspur.

Don Camillo, with the slower cross-country time, was, in accordance with the rules, below Rembrandt, so he was the first of the two to jump. Never a reliable show jumper, he hit one fence, allowing Rembrandt 10 penalties in hand. Unfortunately he failed to rise to the occasion, hit one of the early fences—and then, two from home with victory in sight, he faulted again at the water and so dropped to 3rd place, below Upper Strata.

So Judy Bradwell, a talented and dedicated rider [who for four consecutive years, 1968–1971, won the trophy for the most successful horse trials rider] fulfilled a long-standing ambition by winning Burghley.

1971
EUROPEAN CHAMPIONSHIPS

In 1971 Burghley was once again the venue for the European Championships. Britain's international prestige in the eventing world was very high, English horses and riders had been very successful over the last few years and there was widespread confidence that Burghley would be a well organised competition with a good course. After the World Championships at Punchestown, where only two teams out of six had completed the competition, it was important that the less proficient nations should have their confidence in the sport restored.

It was a very Royal occasion. The Queen and Prince Philip were staying at Burghley House and Princess Anne, who had made such a promising début at the top level when she rode Doublet into 5th place at Badminton in the spring, was one of eight individual riders selected to compete. She was also staying at Burghley—her room was right at the top of one of the towers—and Doublet was housed in solitary splendour in Capability Brown's stables.

But for Princess Anne the auguries were not entirely auspicious; she had recently undergone a fairly serious operation and was not completely fit. She had started riding only three days before Eridge, and there, after leading in the dressage, she had a fall on the cross-country, but still managed the equal fastest time. In spite of the fall the performance gave her confidence that she would be fit to tackle Burghley.

The British team was an outstanding one, consisting of Mary Gordon-Watson and Cornishman V, reigning World Champions as well as the holders of the European title; Richard Meade and The Poacher, winners at

1971. (Left) European Individual Champions, Princess Anne and Doublet. (Right) Team Champions, Great Britain: (left to right) Richard Meade and The Poacher (5th), Mark Phillips and Great Ovation (6th), Debbie West and Baccarat (2nd), Mary Gordon-Watson and Cornishman V (4th).

Badminton in 1970; Mark Phillips and Great Ovation, who had won Badminton in convincing style in the spring, as well as the team trial at Eridge; and Debbie West on Baccarat. Debbie, who had been 3rd at Badminton, was the only newcomer to the team and was a late replacement for Richard Walker whose horse, Upper Strata, had gone lame.

There were six other teams competing. The Russians brought over five horses, four of which were stallions; and other teams came from France, Holland, Italy, Ireland and Switzerland. There were individuals from Sweden and Germany—the Germans would also have sent a team but for last minute injuries to some of their horses, and it might well have provided serious opposition, as the ex-English team horses Chicago and Benson were entered.

Forty-five starters meant two full days of dressage. Princess Anne and Doublet went towards the end of the first day and performed an outstanding test. Both horse and rider were expertly trained by Alison Oliver, and Doublet enjoyed dressage—particularly when he had an audience. Sensing the importance of the occasion, he drew himself up as he came into the arena and became lighter and more responsive. According to Princess Anne he was in an extraordinary frame of mind, for he knew the test and seemed to take a pride in performing the movements well. His score of 41·5 penalties took him into the lead, and to the surprise of his rider he remained there.

Second best test was performed by the Russian horse, Resfeder, ridden by Mr Muhin who was 7·5 points behind Doublet. The Russians acquitted themselves quite well in the dressage but later Mr Elwyn Hartley Edwards commented in *Country Life*: '. . . How strange it is to reflect that a nation that is able to put men into orbit round the moon at the drop of a hat consistently neglects to produce a competent tailor of riding garments. Clothes may not, it is true, make the man, but they improve his over-all outline on a horse.'

Lying 3rd after the dressage were Michel Cochenet and Quaker from France, who had finished 8th in the World Championships at Punchestown. The Poacher and Richard Meade, best of the British team, were equal 6th with 59 penalties, Baccarat was 10th, Cornishman 15th and Great Ovation, whose test was not up to the standard he had achieved at Badminton, was 12th.

At the end of the dressage the British team was leading, a mere 3 points ahead of the Russians, with the French team 3rd, a further 9 points away.

The cross-country course had been given a fairly severe face-lift. The start had been moved to between the arena area and the lake, and there were a large number of new fences. The second Trout Hatchery—a 3 ft. 9 in. step down into the water followed by one of the same height to get out—was brought into the course for the first time. So was the Leaf Pit—a steep drop which caused a lot of comment but proved more impressive to spectators and faint-hearted riders than to the horses. There was a new Coffin at Fence 5, and almost at the end of the course there were two tricky combinations: the Raleigh Round, named in honour of Raleigh who were sponsoring the competition for the first time; and the Serpentine Rails, between the arena and the lake. At both, time could be saved by jumping awkward corners. The course was 4¾ miles long, nearly 1,000 yards longer than the previous year, and the total distance of the speed and endurance test was nearly 18 miles, almost four miles longer than in 1970.

It was a lovely day, sunny and not too hot, and Burghley looked its best in the late summer sunshine. Vast crowds turned up to watch Princess Anne and Doublet, and they were rewarded with a remarkable performance.

Doublet went well on the steeplechase, incurring no penalties, and finished Phase C full of running. Unusually for him, he set out on the cross-country pulling. Princess Anne had been nervous of the big spreads near the beginning of the course, for Doublet was a tidy, intelligent jumper rather than one with enormous scope. However he made little of them, and apart from a stumble coming out of the Trout Hatchery—which did not give his rider a moment's worry although it looked serious to spectators—he was foot perfect throughout the course. It was the second fastest round of the day, and with 18·8 time penalties Princess Anne and Doublet maintained their lead. The only horse to go faster was Classic Chips ridden by Stewart Stevens who scorched round for only 4·4 penalties, which when added to a moderate dressage score left him in 4th place.

Of the British team members, Mary Gordon-Watson, first to go, was under instructions to ride for a safe clear round, and so could not make full use of Cornishman's enormous stride. He went clear, still clocked the fourth fastest time, and at the end of the day was in 3rd place. Baccarat also went extremely well, clear and fractionally faster than Cornishman—quite a feat as Debbie West, having broken a leather, had to ride half the course with one stirrup. He moved up to 2nd place.

The Poacher failed to make the bank coming out of the Trout Hatchery, and so lost 20 penalties in an otherwise good round. He went into 5th place, ahead of Janet Hodgson on Larkspur, riding as an individual, who went clear with 31·2 time penalties.

Great Ovation had a refusal at the corner of the Serpentine Rails, but with a good time was lying 7th at the end of the day. In 8th place was another English individual, Angela Sowden, riding Mooncoin, who also put up a fine performance.

None of the British riders got any penalties on the steeplechase, and only two out of the twelve failed to finish. They seemed to be in a league of their own, for the foreigners on the whole fared badly and from the beginning of the day there never looked to be any threat to the British team.

Best placed of the riders from abroad was Lieutenant A. Buehler from Switzerland riding Wukari, who was lying 9th at the end of the day. Resfeder, who had performed such a good dressage test, finished in 10th place in spite of a fall at the Waterloo Rails and a refusal at the Dairy Farm. He was the best of the Russians, of whom one rider was eliminated and the other two had 100 jumping penalties each.

The Irish team was severely handicapped when their best horse, San Carlos, ridden by Ronnie MacMahon, was found to be lame after the dressage. Of the rest of their team, Ballangarry, ridden by Bill McLernon, went clear and was lying 11th at the end of the day, but Smokey VI and Bill Powell-Harris who had gone so well at Burghley the year before had a fall at the Bull Pens and a refusal at the Trout Hatchery—where Broken Promise and Mrs Willson also had a fall.

Sarajevo, ridden by Jan Jonsson from Sweden—the combination that was to win the individual bronze medal at Munich the following year—also went clear, but a fall on the steeplechase kept him in 12th place.

The cross-country had proved difficult: there were only nine clear

ounds, and ten competitors failed to finish. Trouble was well spread round
he course, but the Trout Hatchery fences caused the most grief—there
were five falls at the first and four at the second where three horses were
also eliminated. The Waterloo Plain fence, the Coffin, the Steps Down and
Up all caused trouble, as did the Serpentine Rails.

At the end of the day the British team had a lead of 400 points over the
French, with the Irish 3rd and the Russians 4th. On the final day the
French had to withdraw Quaker as he had a badly swollen knee, so with
40 points from their discard score added to the total, they slipped to the
back of the team order, behind the Irish, the Russians and the Italians.
Both the Swiss and the Dutch teams were eliminated.

On the final day the position of the British team looked secure, as did
that of Princess Anne. After the jumping the British team finished with a
lead of 422 points, as a total of 71·5 jumping penalties from the Irish team
forfeited their second place to the Russians who all jumped well.

In the individual order, Cornishman slipped a place to 4th when he had
two fences down, allowing Classic Chips, who hit one, to overtake him for
3rd place. Baccarat had 10 penalties, leaving Princess Anne with an even
greater margin for error. She could afford to hit three fences and still win,
but she and Doublet rewarded the tense and excited crowd with a faultless
performance—which was only in keeping, Doublet must have felt, with the
superiority of his performances in the other phases.

It was a fine achievement by Princess Anne who was riding in only her
second major Three-Day Event. She led from the start, and finished 38
points ahead of her nearest rival. Looking back on it seven years later she
said: 'I didn't really understand what it was that I had done', and she felt
that she did not fully appreciate at the time what a good horse Doublet
was.

Side by side with Princess Anne's victory went an equally impressive
win by the British team. All four members were in the first six, and British
riders filled the top eight places.

1972

The successes of the British Three-Day Event team at the Munich
Olympics three weeks earlier must have sparked off new enthusiasm for the
sport: for on cross-country day there was a record number of spectators.

The competition promised to be an interesting one. The individual Gold
Medallist, Richard Meade, was riding Wayfarer (instead of his Olympic
horse Laurieston); and Debbie West and Baccarat, withdrawn from the
team on the morning of dressage day at Munich because of Baccarat's
lameness, were also competing. And hopes were high that Princess Anne—
this year riding the Queen's Columbus as Doublet was out of action—
would repeat her success of the year before. Also there was a strong foreign
entry, with competitors from Canada, Germany, Italy, Holland and
Australia—many of them Olympic reserves.

There was a record number of entries—the list had to be closed at 100—
and a record number of starters: 72. In the dressage, which took two and a
half days, the Germans showed their superiority, with all four of their
riders in the first six. However, pride of place went to Lorna Sutherland
riding Peer Gynt, who kept the home flag flying with a beautiful test, to
head the field 9 points in front of Otto Ammerman and Alpaca. Ammerman just beat his compatriot Kurt Mergler riding Vaibel. Richard Meade,

1972. Janet Hodgson and Larkspur, Burghley's most consistent combination.

lying 4th, was the only other English rider to make any impression on the Germans. In 5th place were Sioux and Horst Karsten, who had been in the German Olympic team but had retired on the cross-country. Though in Munich, Sioux had led the dressage, his test at Burghley was disappointing. Princess Anne rode Columbus tactfully, to go into 8th place.

In the final order, the dressage leaders were generally eclipsed—with the cross-country exerting a decisive influence: there were only fifteen clean rounds, and a large number—twenty-six—were eliminated or retired.

The course, which was fairly challenging, was a modified and shortened version of that used for the European Championships. The fences at the Trout Hatcheries took a big toll just as they had the previous year. Eight riders were treated to a ducking at one or the other, and there were rumours—later proved entirely false—of a hole in the bottom of the upper one. Barbara Hammond riding Eagle Rock had the distinction of falling at both water obstacles and achieved uncalled-for fame, as one of her duckings—the 'prang of the day'—was shown over and over again on BBC TV. The Coffin, the Rails in Gully over the ditch below the arenas, and the Serpentine Rails, unaltered from 1971, also caused considerable trouble.

Speed proved to be the decisive factor. The fastest round—only eight time penalties—put Janet Hodgson and Larkspur into the lead, taking them up from 11th place. Larkspur, aged twelve, had been on the short list for the Olympic team, and this was his third notable performance in three successive years at Burghley. Bred in Ireland and a stayer rather than a sprinter, Larkspur made no mistakes at the fences. But his rider had an anxious moment when they caught up with the horse ahead of them (Knowlton Corona ridden by Oliver Fox-Pitt) at the Dairy Farm. Janet did not take a check, though, and the two horses jumped the fences with only a length between them.

Baccarat, only one point behind Larkspur in the dressage, achieved the second fastest time on the cross-country, to finish the day in 2nd place. Breathing down their necks was Hazel Booth on Mary Poppins II, a mare who had a very good record in One-Day Events and who had come 8th at Badminton in the spring.

Lucinda Prior-Palmer and Be Fair (whose sire Fair and Square had won Burghley in 1968) having shared 11th place with Larkspur in the dressage, went well across country for 10·4 time penalties, the third fastest time. They would have gone into 2nd place but for an expensive 2·4 penalties on the steeplechase which kept them below Mary Poppins. It was Lucinda's first ride at Burghley; the previous year she and Be Fair had been in the team for the Junior European Championships; and this spring they had been 5th at Badminton. Her future partner, George, was also having his first run at Burghley (ridden by Matthew Straker, his owner's son) but he had a fall on the steeplechase and a refusal on the cross-country. Princess Anne disappointed her many supporters when, finding Columbus too strong for her on the steeplechase, she pulled up and failed to appear on the cross-country.

Richard Meade with Wayfarer couldn't quite match the girls for speed but went well to end the day in 5th place. He was the only one of the dressage leaders not to slide down the order. Peer Gynt had two refusals and, with the exception of Sioux, who had a slow clear round to drop to 9th place, the Germans all got into difficulties. Alpaca retired after a number of refusals, and Vaibel had a fall at the Rails in the Gully. Bill Roycroft, the veteran Australian who had come 6th in the Olympics on Warrathoola, was the best of the overseas riders, taking Harley—later to be ridden by Sue Hatherly—into 6th place.

On the final day Harley was spun by the vets, as they considered him to be lame—much to the chagrin of his rider—and so was PJLL Esq, ridden by John Smart, who had been lying 7th. Those in the lower placings automatically moved up.

Five points covered the first four horses—less than the cost of a fence down—so nerves were taut by the time the last few horses were due to go. The first four all went clear, though Larkspur, who in the words of his rider 'didn't think show jumps were really worth jumping', was lucky, as he hit two fences hard and only just cleared the water. Wayfarer incurred 10 penalties, but could afford them without losing his place—so the order stayed the same as it had been overnight, with Larkspur a worthy winner and Baccarat runner-up for the second successive year.

1973

In 1973 Burghley was held from 30th August to 2nd September—earlier than usual, as the European Championships at Kiev in the USSR were scheduled for the following week.

There were fifty-two starters, a more manageable number as far as the organization was concerned than the seventy-two of the previous year.

Among them were eight competitors from overseas and it was one of these, a 21-year-old French girl Martine Pfister, riding Ugoline, who surprised everyone by taking the lead in the dressage, just ahead of Mark Phillips on Maid Marion. Maid Marion was owned jointly by Bertie Hill, team Gold Medallist in the Olympics in 1956, and his son Tony, her usual rider, who had just come out of hospital having been consigned there with a badly injured back from a fall off the mare at Osberton. Mark Phillips had in the past helped Tony Hill with the training of Maid Marion but only rode her with Burghley in mind a few days before it began.

Third after the dressage was Lorna Sutherland, who gave her usual high class performance with Peer Gynt. Chris Collins on Centurian was 4th, 15 points behind the leader.

At 3¾ miles the cross-country course was shorter than usual, but it was treated with considerable respect by riders when they walked round. It started in a different direction—towards the road between Stamford and the stables, a part of the park not used since 1966; and there were a number of new fences. On the new loop there was a very attractive sleeper-roofed Pig Sty, and into the Leaf Pit there were some imposing new rails with a steep drop on landing.

The dressage marks had been fairly well spread out, but some spectacular gains in the order were still made by those who went fast across country. The biggest improvement of all was accomplished by Smokey VI and Bill Powell-Harris from Limerick. With his enormous stride Smokey made light of the cross-country and finished not only with no time penalties—the only horse to do so—but 30 seconds within the time. A poor performance in the dressage had left him in 39th place, but after the cross-country he moved up to 5th.

Diana Thorne and her grey seven-year-old, The Kingmaker, on whom she had won the Midland Bank Novice Championships in 1972, made almost as great an improvement as Smokey. A successful point-to-point jockey (she was later the first lady to win a race under National Hunt Rules) Diana rode with great dash across country and returned the second fastest time to move from 29th after the dressage to 3rd place. It was a performance full of promise for the future. Katy Hill and Day Return also went extremely fast to pull up to 4th. Centurian did not really like the firm going on the steeplechase, incurring 8 penalties there, and with 24·4 more on the cross-country he finished the day in 6th place.

Harley, who had gone so well for the Australian Olympic rider Bill Roycroft the year before, went no less well for his new rider, Sue Hatherly; with only 8·4 time penalties they finished the day in 2nd place. And Sue gave further evidence of her skill across country when on her other horse, Devil's Jump, she went only slightly more slowly to move into 7th place.

Maid Marion, at the age of eight, was a fairly experienced cross-country horse. She had been successful in junior competitions with Tony Hill, finishing second in the individual at the Junior European Championships at Eridge the previous year. At Badminton in the spring she had been eliminated at the Coffin. At Burghley, Mark Phillips could not persuade her to attack the first few fences with any enthusiasm, for she seemed to lack confidence after her recent fall. But with a considerable amount of encouragement from her rider she became more trusting as the round progressed, and by the end was jumping well. In spite of the early difficulties they clocked a good time and took the lead. When Ugoline had a

refusal at the Coffin and another at the rails into the Leaf Pit, Maid Marion was left with a 14-point lead over Harley.

As it turned out, the Coffin caused the most trouble—as Coffins usually do—three horses were eliminated there and ten others refused. At the Waterloo Rails, a formidable drop fence, three horses fell and four refused, and at the Leaf Pit Rails eight horses refused and one was eliminated. These fences took the lion's share of the trouble and for once the Trout Hatchery—or 'Drought Hatchery' as it was aptly misprinted in a newspaper—caused few problems. Seventeen horses went clear and thirteen failed to complete the cross-country.

On the final day, five horses were withdrawn, among them Devil's Jump, who failed to pass the veterinary panel. The ensuing show jumping was full of drama. It was a difficult course and only nine of the thirty-four horses who were left in the competition jumped clear.

The order changed to such a degree that Jane Starkey on Acrobat, lying 10th after the cross-country, and Lorna Sutherland on Peer Gynt lying 9th (they had one refusal on the cross-country) each gained four places when they jumped clear, to finish 6th and 5th respectively.

Centurian made no mistakes, and moved up from 6th to 4th. From then on the pressure was on the leaders. Smokey, next to go, was over-excited, incurred 21 penalties, and so dropped in the final order to 8th. But worse was to follow, for Katy Hill had an unfortunate fall at the very last fence and with 44·25 penalties dropped to 11th. The Kingmaker, lying 3rd, went clear and so changed places with Harley when he had one fence down.

Maid Marion, with a fence in hand, jumped well until the last obstacle. There Mark Phillips—distracted by memories of the Mini-Munich Event in 1971 when he had been in the lead after the cross-country and had fallen at the last fence in the show jumping—mistimed the take off and Maid Marion ploughed through it. To her rider she never felt like falling, though to the spectators the flailing poles seemed like a repetition of Katy Hill's disaster. But it only gave them 10 penalties and so Mark Phillips and Maid Marion were the winners, with Diana Thorne and The Kingmaker the runners-up.

1974
WORLD
CHAMPIONSHIPS

For the Americans the 1974 World Championships brought to a triumphant conclusion a long period of dedication and hard work, during which they had played second fiddle to the British. They showed their superiority with a convincing win in the team competition, and two American riders, Bruce Davidson and Michael Plumb, won the individual gold and silver medals. Their win brought about a change in the league of eventing nations. The commanding position of the British, unchallenged from 1967 to 1972, had been eroded the previous year at the European Championships at Kiev. After Burghley we were no longer the top eventing nation. The Americans (who had won the team silver medal at the last three Olympics) were not yet in a completely commanding position, as they had only the World, and no Olympic, titles to their credit, but for them Burghley represented a major step up the ladder.

It was an occasion that aroused great excitement in the equestrian world—a genuine World Championship meeting with nearly all the best eventing nations competing. Teams came from ten countries and individuals from two more. Spectators flocked to Burghley—it was estimated that over the four days the crowd reached the 100,000 mark—and the arrival of a large number of visitors from abroad posed considerable problems for the organisers, as accommodation in the area was (and still is) limited. Brigadier Grose had left nothing to chance, carrying out a full-scale rehearsal of all his helpers the previous week, and the organisation received widespread praise for the masterly way in which it coped with the crowds.

The Selectors had a difficult time in finalising their choice for the British team from the six riders who had been training at Ascot. In the end they chose Richard Meade on Wayfarer, one of the few horses to go well in Kiev; Chris Collins on Smokey VI; Bridget Parker on Cornish Gold, who had been in the Gold Medal-winning team at Munich two years before; and Columbus ridden by Mark Phillips, whose claims for the team were undisputed as he had won Badminton in impressive style in the spring.

1974. World Team Champions, the USA: (left to right) Michael Plumb and Good Mixture (2nd), Denny Emerson and Victor Dakin (14th), Don Sachey and Plain Sailing (21st), Bruce Davidson and Irish Cap (1st).

Janet Hodgson on Larkspur, who had been second at Badminton, and Lucinda Prior-Palmer on Be Fair, rode as individuals with five other English competitors including Princess Anne on Goodwill.

Altogether there were fifty-eight competitors, and the dressage judges had to wait until almost the end of the second day to see the best test. It was performed by the Russian stallion Tost ridden by Vladimir Laniugin, an army corporal, for a score of 42·33 penalties. The German mare Virginia, ridden by Martin Plewa, and Bruce Davidson on Irish Cap, were equal second with 45·67. Irish Cap had amply illustrated his class by finishing third at Badminton—and as if English riders were not already fully aware of the threat from this direction, Davidson had poured salt on the wound by winning the standard Three-Day Event at Bramham two weeks before Burghley, on his wife's horse Paddy.

Of the English entries the best test was performed by Barbara Hammond riding Eagle Rock. They went into 6th place, and Janet Hodgson on Larkspur was 8th, a fraction of a point behind. Columbus, less relaxed than he had been at Badminton, scored 55·67, putting him into 10th place. Cornish Gold was 31st, Smokey 25th and Wayfarer with a score of 58·37 shared 16th place with the American team captain Michael Plumb on Good Mixture.

At the end of the dressage the marks were very close. Counting the best three scores the Germans were leading with 160·33, the U.S.A. were 2nd with 169, France was 3rd with 172·67, and Britain was 4th with 175.

By general consensus the cross-country course was considered to be an excellent one. It was very big, but it was beautifully presented, and in order to reduce the advantage to the Burghley regulars among the competitors, it consisted very largely of new fences. The Double Coffin in the ditch below the arena was an interesting innovation, as were the awkward Zig-Zag Rails over a wide ditch in a steep-sided dip in the ground. There were awe-inspiring drops at the Dairy Farm Mound and at the Waterloo Rails, the latter causing five falls. But it was the Trout Hatchery that was the most influential fence, as it so often has been. With a steep downhill approach there were rails of 3 ft. 3 in.—which Bill Thomson says he made bigger than he thought they should have been, as he expected (wrongly as it turned out) that the technical delegate would have them lowered. Here there were eight eliminations, five falls and six refusals.

A challenging course as far as the fences were concerned, it was also a serious test of fitness and stamina. The steeplechase was 2 miles 633 yards long, and to finish within the time the horses had to gallop for 5 minutes 30 seconds—about 30 seconds longer than for an average Three-Day Event. The cross-country was $4\frac{3}{4}$ miles, the same as in 1971, and roughly half a mile longer than usual. Also, on cross-country day the warm slightly humid, atmosphere—which added greatly to the enjoyment of the spectators—did not help the horses; Larkspur was affected by it and so were Wayfarer and Smokey. Fifteen horses jumped clear, fourteen were eliminated, and one retired.

None of the first team members completed the course without jumping penalties, but Bridget Parker made only one mistake, at the Bull Pens, and finished in a good time. The first German and French horses to go were both eliminated, and the American Don Sachey, on Plain Sailing (who had gone clear in the 1966 World Championships when ridden by Rosemary Kopanski), had a fall at the Sleeper Wall and Bank.

1974. World Individual Champions, Bruce Davidson and Irish Cap.

The first clear round came from an English individual, Hugh Thomas, riding Playamar. Playamar, aged 8, had gone well at Badminton, finishing 8th. At Burghley he looked very impressive over the fences, and with what turned out to be the second fastest time he was lying 4th at the end of the cross-country.

With the second team riders, things looked slightly less encouraging for the British. Smokey, normally a cast-iron certainty to go well across country, had two crashing falls—one when he tried to bank the log pile and the other at the Waterloo Rails—but still finished the course in a reasonable time. Virginia for Germany went clear, but with more than twice as many time faults as Smokey his challenge for the Individual evaporated. More serious for the British was the fact that Victor Dakin and Denny

Emerson went very well, as is related elsewhere, in the same time as Chris Collins and Smokey.

Then Larkspur, although he felt slightly unenthusiastic to his rider, put up his usual good performance for 30·8 time penalties and 5th place.

With the third batch of team riders, both Switzerland and Italy were put out of the competition when their riders were eliminated. For Germany, Herbert Blocker and Albrant, 2nd in Kiev, had 20 penalties at the Zig-Zag Rails. Then Columbus gave a superb performance—although he had an awkward moment at the Trout Hatchery—in the fastest time of the day. It was a classic round from a brilliant rider and an exceptional horse; Mark Phillips's extraordinary ability to ride at consuming speed across country combined perfectly with Columbus's devouring stride and enormous scope and agility.

But those who were watching at the finish could see that something was wrong, for one of the grey's hind legs seemed to be almost useless. The extent of the damage was not immediately known, and most of the spectators' attention was fixed on the next competitors. Following Columbus was Irish Cap, who had a better dressage score and was also going extremely well—but he could not match Columbus's racing speed, and taking 45 seconds longer he ended the day in 2nd place, 8 points behind.

There were then two clear rounds from English individuals. Lucinda Prior-Palmer and Be Fair, who on the steeplechase had gone through the wrong channel at the start of the second circuit, thus incurring 28 penalties, clocked a good time on the cross-country to go into 13th place. Toby Sturgis on Demi-Douzaine, who went slightly slower on the cross-country, moved up to 8th. Goodwill and Princess Anne had one refusal coming out of the Double Coffin in an otherwise good round.

There was uncertainty about the team positions, for rumours were circulating about the condition of Columbus. When the fourth German horse, Sioux, ridden by Horst Karsten, had an uncharacteristic lapse and refused twice at the Double Coffin, it was clear that Germany would not take the lead. Bothar Bui and Ronnie MacMahon from Ireland went clear, but there was no redemption for the Irish team, who had started with only three horses, two of whom already had incurred 100 jumping penalties.

Then the final British rider, Richard Meade, returned a much-needed clear round on Wayfarer. At this stage of his career Wayfarer was not a fast horse and incurred 47·2 time penalties. Following him, Good Mixture, who had been 5th at Munich when ridden by Kevin Freeman, achieved a beautiful round in a very fast time to go into 3rd place. Tost from Russia lost his dressage lead with two refusals and no less than 159 time penalties.

Good Mixture's score was good enough to put the Americans in the lead: with a team total of 258 points they had an advantage of 34 points over the British, if Columbus were to be included. Should the discard score, Smokey's 220·2 penalties, replace that of Columbus, the British team total would be 448·60, which was still comfortably ahead of the Germans on 499·53. The Irish were lying 4th, the Russians 5th and the Polish team 6th. Switzerland, France and Austria failed to get three riders round, and all four members of the Italian team were eliminated.

Columbus was found to have displaced a tendon in his hock and so could not jump on the final day. A careful show jumper, he would have had a very good chance of keeping the Americans at bay in the individual honours. So Mark Phillips tragically missed the opportunity of becoming

World Champion (and twice winner at Burghley). For the Queen, who owned and bred Columbus, it was also a grave disappointment.

In the show jumping most of the top half of the field went clear, and there were no changes in the team order. But there was less than one point between the top three horses, so when Playamar jumped clear the pressure was on the Americans. However, though at Munich they had all incurred faults in the show jumping, now, two years later, they looked extremely polished, and the two leaders made no mistakes.

So Bruce Davidson and Irish Cap were the new World Champions, and Michael Plumb and Good Mixture the runners-up. It was a far cry from the World Championships of 1966 when only one of the six American competitors had finished—Kevin Freeman on M'Lord Connolly—and the team had been eliminated.

Thus ended a memorable and exciting competition, with the United States team very worthy winners. There was some consolation for the British in Playamar's third place and from the gallant Larkspur who came fourth.

1975

In the spring, Badminton had been cancelled, so with the Olympics less than a year away Burghley acquired a new importance, affording an opportunity for riders to catch the eye of the Selectors. The week before, the British had met with mixed fortunes in the European Championships at Luhmühlen. Lucinda Prior-Palmer and Be Fair had carried off the Individual Gold Medal, and Princess Anne had been runner-up; but the team, which had been in the lead after the cross-country, had to yield to the Russians when Sue Hatherly on Harley had a fall in the show jumping.

At Burghley the FEI's new Three-Day Event Dressage Test was performed, replacing the time-honoured version used here since 1964. The movements to be executed were similar—among them canter to halt, half pass and counter canter—but there was a difference in the paces that the horses were required to show. The collected, ordinary and extended paces of the old test were replaced with working, medium and extended movements in the new one.

The best test was performed by Rachel Bayliss on Gurgle the Greek, a talented dressage horse who was (at the time of going to press still is) almost unbeatable in One-Day Horse Trials but had yet to prove himself in Three-Day Events. Five points behind was Aly Pattinson on Olivia, who started her career as a show hack and then competed in dressage competitions before being turned to eventing. Aly Pattinson underlined her skill in this phase by riding into 7th place (16.34 points behind the leader) her other horse, Alex Colquhoun's Carawich, on whom she had won the Midland Bank Championships the year before. Touch and Go, ridden by Miranda Frank, also went well to move into 3rd place.

For the first time in the history of the Burghley Trials, Bill Thomson had not designed the cross-country course. He was taking a year's 'sabbatical', and Colonel Henry Nicoll, who had been a member of the course inspection panel in 1972 and 1973, and who had wide experience of building One-Day Event courses, was standing in for him.

The course had a new look; it was a big but inviting, and there were a number of new fences. Among them were the Sunken Trakehner which worried the competitors when they walked the course; the Maze—so called because there were a number of alternative ways of jumping it; and a most attractive new thatched Boat House beside the lake. The course, which earned widespread praise, was very lavishly finished; on one fence alone —Fence 25, the Spruce Fence out of Chabonel Spinney—almost one hundred Christmas trees were used for filling.

Out of fifty-two starters, nineteen went clear and twenty-one, or 41 per cent, failed to finish—a much higher percentage than in the years either immediately before or in those since, when Bill Thomson built the courses.

The difficult fences—the Double Coffin, the Trakehner and the Trout Hatchery—came early on, and once through the Trout Hatchery most competitors completed the course with no further difficulty.

The first horse to go, Favour, ridden by John Kersley, jumped clear and finished within the time, to make the course look deceptively easy. Favour was one of no less than eight horses who incurred no time penalties on the cross-country—for the going was exceptionally fast—and finished the day with no addition to their dressage scores. Both Pat Biden on Little Extra, who went into 5th place, and Katie O'Hara from Northern Ireland on Village Gossip (3rd), later to be ridden by Lucinda Prior-Palmer, came into this category, and both looked impressive over the fences.

The dressage leaders got into difficulties; Gurgle the Greek—who had achieved a kind of fame when he went underneath the rail of a trakehner at Badminton—confirmed his dislike of this kind of obstacle when he refused twice at the Sunken Trakehner; and Olivia jumped too big over the log into

1975. Aly Pattinson and Carawich over the Ermine Street Log Wall.

the Trout Hatchery, capsized on landing and gave Aly Pattinson a duck-ing. Touch and Go went well but incurred 21·6 time penalties to slip one place to 4th.

Richard Meade had been without a top-class horse since the retirement of Wayfarer after the World Championships in 1974. At Burghley he was riding Tommy Buck, who was competing at the invitation of the Selection Committee as he was not fully qualified. After the dressage they were 12th, and Meade displayed all his old mastery in nursing his inexperienced horse round the cross-country. They survived an anxious moment when Tommy Buck almost became straddled on the log at the Trout Hatchery, and finished with only 2·4 time penalties to go into 2nd place.

Janet Hodgson, who had been injured in her two falls from Larkspur at Luhmühlen, had offered Mark Phillips a last-minute ride on her young mare, Gretna Green. In an eventful round they recovered from being almost completely submerged when Gretna Green 'bellyflopped' at the Trout Hatchery; and almost came to grief when she banked a hedge in the Maze; but they kept going and finished in 6th place with 7·2 time penalties.

Right at the end of the day Aly Pattinson, having changed into dry clothes, completed a superb round on Carawich to take over the lead. Undaunted by her immersion in the Trout Hatchery, she had gained confidence from the manner in which Olivia, who was relatively inexperienced, had tackled the fences; and on Carawich she kept up a relentless rhythm, taking few checks and wasting little time at the fences. At the age of seven Carawich already looked a seasoned and expert cross-country horse.

The marks were very close, and on the final day the order changed considerably. Acrobat, ridden by Jane Starkey who had come to grief on her other horse in attempting the shortest route at the Maze, moved up from 11th place to 6th as a result of a clear round. Little Extra, with 10 penalties, dropped two places to 7th, and Touch and Go dropped one to 5th. Favour jumped clear to move from 7th to 4th, and the most dramatic climb of all came from Mark Phillips who rose from 6th to 2nd as a result of a clear round on Gretna Green. An expensive 20 penalties caused Village Gossip to drop five places to 8th, and Richard Meade slipped to 3rd when Tommy Buck hit one fence. Carawich could still afford no more than one fence down. Never the most reliable of show jumpers, he needed the margin, for he hit the middle element of the treble—but the Raleigh Trophy and the £750 first prize were his.

The horses filling the first four places were all seven-year-olds, which promised well for the future. Aly Pattinson and Carawich staked their claim to consideration by the Selectors, and Richard Meade and Mark Phillips both offered further proof of their extraordinary ability to succeed with a wide variety of horses.

1976

The drought during the long hot summer had left the grass in many areas completely scorched, but the rain came in time to freshen the green of the park at Burghley. The dressage took place in blustery weather, which seemed inhospitable after the endless succession of perfect days and dampened the enthusiasm of spectators and competitors alike. Horse Trials enthusiasts were also depressed by the misfortunes of the team at the Olympics, where two of the British horses had to be withdrawn after the cross-country thus causing the elimination of the team.

The best dressage test was performed by Captain Mark Phillips on Persian Holiday, who had been on the short list for the Olympic team and had won the final team trial at Osberton. The two German competitors, Horst Karsten riding Cavalier and Martin Plewa on Habicht, were equal 2nd, only one point behind. With only 14 points separating the first twelve horses the dressage did not have very much significance in the final results.

For cross-country day the sun reappeared and Burghley regained its charms. Because the going on the golf course had been extremely hard, the organisers had decided two weeks before to move the steeplechase course to Waterloo Plain where the going would be better as the fields were partly stubble and partly cut kale and could be harrowed if necessary. After the decision had been made, a considerable amount of rain had fallen, and with more heavy rain the night before, on cross-country day the going was deep. Also the confined space necessitated a tight circuit and each horse had to complete three laps. It was therefore difficult to do a good time on the steeplechase and it exerted more influence than usual, both because competitors had more penalties, and because it had a tiring effect on the horses and may have caused riders to go more slowly on the cross-country.

The course proved to be well within the capabilities of most of the competitors, for only four horses were eliminated. Four more retired and there were eight falls. Twenty-eight of the sixty starters incurred no jumping penalties. Speed therefore became the crucial factor, both on the steeplechase and on the cross-country, especially as the dressage marks were close.

First to go was Jane Holderness-Roddam, who as Jane Bullen had won Badminton in 1968 and in the same year had been a member of the Gold Medal-winning team at the Mexico Olympics. She was riding Warrior, a nine-year-old bay gelding by Warwick (sire also of The Kingmaker), whose owner, Mrs Suzy Howard lived in the USA and had come over to watch her horse perform at Burghley. Warrior was lying 13th after the dressage. On the steeplechase he incurred 9·6 penalties—a disappointment to his rider who was used to carefully timing herself to finish within the time—and finished exhausted, though he recovered by the end of Phase C.

Competing in his first major Three-Day Event, and having had a fall at Bramham earlier in the year, Warrior was not pushed round the cross-country. He gave Jane a very good ride, jumping sensibly and carefully, and finished with 18·4 time penalties. As the day progressed it became clear that Warrior's time on the steeplechase would stand him in good stead, and only three horses were to go faster. His total score put him in the lead and he remained there until the end of the day, when Demi-Douzaine, ridden by Toby Sturgis—who at the time was suffering from brucellosis—raced round in the fastest time of all to snatch the lead by one point.

Mark Phillips and Persian Holiday looked set to go well into the lead, for they had only 8·8 time faults on the steeplechase; but at the Coffin, Persian Holiday attempted to jump the rails after the ditch without putting in a stride, did not quite make it, and ejected his rider from the saddle. In spite of the fall they still managed the fourth fastest time on the cross-country and finished the day in 12th place.

Welton Samaritan, ridden by John Kersley, moved up to 3rd place after the second fastest cross-country round. Lying 4th was Sandra Brookes on Welton Playboy, who like Welton Samaritan was a son of Welton Gameful. Lucinda Prior-Palmer riding Killaire was 5th, having clocked the same

1976. Jane Holderness-Roddam and Warrior clear the Diamonds.

cross-country time as John Kersley. Lucinda, whose horse Be Fair had gone lame in Montreal, had been riding Killaire only since her return from the Olympics.

At the end of the day the only placed horses to have been in the first ten in the dressage were Copper Tiger ridden by Carolan Geekie (7th) and Jane Starkey's Topper Too (8th). The Germans went too slowly to maintain their challenge.

On the final day, Welton Samaritan was withdrawn, so everyone lower than 3rd moved up one place. The show jumping was full of drama; there were not many clear rounds and the placings changed considerably. The first upset occurred when Elizabeth Boone and Felday Farmer, having climbed from near the bottom in the dressage to 6th place as a result of a very fast cross-country round, slipped back to 12th after hitting four fences.

With a clear round, Persian Holiday moved up four places to 8th, and Topper Too, who also went clear, moved up to 4th. Welton Playboy had one fence down—in the end he remained in 3rd place—and was overtaken by Killaire who jumped clear. Warrior, only one point behind the leader, gave his supporters an anxious moment when his breastplate broke and trailed round his legs. His rider, with visions of his breaking a leg, had to keep grabbing it—but, undaunted, Warrior cleared all the fences. Toby

Sturgis then had to jump clear to win the Raleigh Trophy—but the suspense was soon dispelled, for he hit the second fence, and faulted again later.

So Jane Holderness-Roddam joined the select band of riders who have won both Badminton and Burghley. Lucinda Prior-Palmer and Mr Cyzer's Killaire were 2nd, and Sandra Brookes and Welton Playboy, the least experienced of the prizewinners, 3rd. Toby Sturgis and Demi-Douzaine moved down to 5th—which seemed a harsh punishment after such a good cross-country performance.

1977
EUROPEAN
CHAMPIONSHIPS

The 1977 European Championships were held in England by virtue of Lucinda Prior-Palmer's victory at Luhmühlen two years earlier. This title was the only one still retained in Britain, as the Americans had captured the Olympic and the World Championship titles, and the Russians were the reigning European Team Champions. It was therefore important that things should go well at Burghley.

The prospects for the team were not improved by the last-minute withdrawal of Mark Phillips, whose horse Persian Holiday was not completely fit. Nevertheless it was a good team, consisting of Jane Holderness-Roddam and Warrior, winners at Burghley in 1976, Lucinda Prior-Palmer on her Badminton winner, Mrs Straker's George, Chris Collins riding Smokey and Clarissa Strachan with Merry Sovereign—brought in to replace Mark Phillips.

The most serious danger clearly came from the Germans, who had as their ace card their Olympic bronze medallist Karl Schultz, on Madrigal. The Russian team had no readily recognisable names other than Araks ridden by Victor Kalinin, who had been 6th at Luhmühlen and had completed the course in Montreal. Teams came also from France, Poland, Ireland and Italy; and individuals from Holland and Switzerland.

Throughout the Event Burghley was blessed with beautiful weather, and over the four days an estimated crowd of 80,000 came to watch—more than for any year other than the 1974 World Championships. The grey-gold stone of the house looked especially beautiful against the vivid green of the grass, for it had been a wet summer and the grass had drawn strength from the rain.

As expected, the Germans dominated the dressage, occupying four of the top seven places. Madrigal opened up a resounding lead—just as he had done in Montreal—with a superb performance that incurred only 21 penalties. Another member of the German team, Hannah Huppelsberg-Zwock, a geriatric nurse by profession, and the first girl to ride in a German Three-Day Event team, came second on Akzent, 10 points behind her compatriot. Lucinda Prior-Palmer, benefiting from her dressage training in Germany earlier in the year, gave a polished performance on George to go into 3rd place, a daunting 10·75 points behind Madrigal. A German individual competitor, Otto Ammerman on Volturno, was 4th. In 5th place was the only Russian to perform a creditable test—Anton Trubitsyn riding a grey stallion, Propeller.

At the end of the dressage the German team was leading, with a total for the best three of 87·5; and Britain was 2nd, 21 points behind. The Russians were 3rd with 131 penalties.

Cautious optimism was the mood in the British camp after the dressage.

The team horses had all gone well and the scores were mostly very close—between 35 and 50. The multiplying factor had been set at 0·75, as the technical delegate considered that the cross-country course was relatively easy. The British riders felt that the resulting telescoping of the dressage scores was in their favour, as it reduced the advantage of the Germans; but the fact that the cross-country course was easy was a disadvantage.

On cross-country day the going was perfect. Inexplicably, the steeple-chase, which was the same length as in 1975, exerted an unusual influence, and six horses failed to make the start of Phase D. Indeed the steeplechase took a far heavier toll than the cross-country, on which only two horses were eliminated and all the rest finished. Out of 41 starters there were 21 clear rounds—the highest percentage ever—and only 6 falls.

With the dressage marks close and the fences causing little trouble it was clear that speed would be the key factor, especially as the course was very long—4¾ miles. Chris Collins and Smokey, the first of the British team to go, were the only ones to complete a clear round within the optimum time, and with nothing to add to their 40 dressage penalties they finished the day in 4th place. It was an encouraging start for the British team—especially since Akzent, the first of the German team to go, had a refusal at Capability's Cutting, and incurred numerous time penalties.

There followed two good performances from English individuals. Aly Adsetts (née Pattinson) on Carawich, winners at Burghley in 1975, added 20·4 time penalties to a good dressage score to take 7th place; and Diana Thorne on The Kingmaker put up the fourth fastest time of the day to move up to 5th.

None of the second team members had clear rounds. The German horse El Paso, ridden by Harry Klugman, retired on the steeplechase, as did Blue Tom Tit ridden by Van der Vater for Ireland. The Russian horse Propeller had a refusal at the Half Coffin and a fall at the last fence, and Merry Sovereign refused at the Double Coffin.

Then Karl Schultz gave a very impressive performance, wasting no time, to put himself in an unbeatable position as far as the cross-country was concerned. Cambridge Blue, ridden by John Watson from Ireland went even faster—incurring only 0·8 of a time fault—but because of his poor dressage score could go no higher than 8th place at the end of the day. Warrior also went extremely well for 10·4 penalties and 6th place.

By the time the last horses from each team were ready to go the outcome was by no means certain and not everyone realized that Schultz was in an unbeatable position.

The fourth member of the German team was Horst Karsten riding Sioux who had been left out of the team for Montreal as the horse was considered unreliable and, at the age of thirteen, past his best. Earlier in 1977 he had won the German Championships at Luhmühlen, proving that at one year older he was still a horse to be reckoned with—and in October he was to win also at Boekelo in Holland. At Burghley he clocked the third fastest time on the cross-country and moved up from 7th after the dressage to 3rd place, 9·2 points behind Madrigal.

Excitement was sustained throughout the day, for Lucinda Prior-Palmer and George were the very last to go. It was with horror that Lucinda's enormous crowd of supporters learned that she had fallen on the steeple-chase. When it was announced that she had incurred no penalties, disbelief set in, but it proved to be the case, for she had fallen outside the penalty

zone and had made a remarkably quick recovery. A brilliant cross-country round for only 5·6 time penalties put George into 2nd place.

At the end of the speed and endurance the British team had taken over the lead, 40 points ahead of the Germans. The Irish, who had three riders with clear rounds on the cross-country, were a further 66 points behind. The French were 4th, the Russians 5th and the Poles 6th. The Italians, who had only entered three riders in the first place, were eliminated.

On the final day, Merry Sovereign, having been badly cut, was withdrawn, so there was no margin for error, and the British team riders were not over confident.

The team position looked slightly precarious when Smokey had two fences down, but although they proved expensive to him (dropping him in the order from 4th to 7th), as far as the team was concerned they were more than compensated for by Akzent's 30 penalties. Then The Kingmaker jumped clear to threaten the leaders.

Karl Schultz came into the ring, doubtless haunted by memories of Montreal, when, in a similar position, Madrigal had hit two fences and forfeited the Gold Medal. The tension was great, for everyone realized that he only had to hit one fence to give Lucinda a chance of the title. He did just that, then Sioux, lying 3rd, also had 10 penalties, before Warrior rounded off a good performance with a clear round to finish in 5th place.

George, last of all to go, treated the spectators to a nerve-wracking few minutes, but to their great delight made no mistakes and wrested the title from Germany. Madrigal was 2nd, Sioux 3rd and The Kingmaker 4th.

The team order stayed the same as it had been overnight, with Great Britain the triumphant winners, the Germans 2nd and the Irish 3rd.

For Lucinda Prior-Palmer, one of the greatest horse trials riders there has ever been, it was a most remarkable achievement. No other rider in history has won two individual European Championships, and no-one else has won Badminton and Burghley in the same year.

With these successes in both the team and individual competitions, eventing in England received a much-needed tonic: but there was no room for complacency, for it was still the Americans who represented the greatest threat to a revival of supremacy.

Nearly but Not Quite

Diana Thorne and The Kingmaker, who were runners-up at Burghley in 1973 and 4th in 1977.

In 1974 Mark Phillips and Columbus had the World Championship within their grasp, but because of injury Columbus was withdrawn on the last day.

Virginia Freeman-Jackson competing in the 1966 World Championships. Riding Sam Weller, she was a member of the winning Irish team and finished 3rd in the individual competition.

Debbie West and Baccarat, twice runners-up at Burghley: in the 1971 European Championships and in 1972.

Hugh Thomas and Playamar, who saved face for the British in the 1974 World Championships by taking 3rd place, less than one point behind the winners.

Facts and Figures

- According to the statistics, you are most likely to win at Burghley if you are under twenty-six, female and ride a bay gelding of eight years old or more. In the last ten years it has been won by men on only two occasions—Mark Phillips in 1973, and Bruce Davidson in 1974. Before that, however, it was only once won by a girl—Anneli Drummond-Hay—in 1961. With the exception of Richard Meade, Bruce Davidson and Captain Harry Freeman-Jackson, all the male winners have been serving army officers.

- Nearly all the winners have been well-established, experienced and dedicated riders. Among the recent winners, riding has generally been their main occupation, though Jane Holderness-Roddam, when she won on Warrior was working part time at the Middlesex Hospital, and in 1971 Princess Anne was also occupied with numerous public duties.

- Captain Edy Goldman has played an important part in the training and basic schooling of a number of riders who have been successful at Burghley. Sheila Willcox, Lorna Sutherland, Debbie West, Judy Bradwell and Angela Tucker all acknowledge a debt to him.

- Seven of the winning riders were also Badminton Champions: Anneli Drummond-Hay, James Templer, Sheila Willcox, Richard Meade, Mark Phillips, Jane Holderness-Roddam and Lucinda Prior-Palmer. But only four horses have won both competitions: Merely-a-Monarch, M'Lord Connolly, George and Warrior. No rider has won Burghley twice.

- The only complete outsider to win was Lorna Sutherland on Popadom. Richard Meade, Princess Anne and James Templer were all outsiders in the sense that they beat people senior to themselves, but they all had some form behind them. Both Don Camillo and Maid Marion were surprise winners, but both had exceptional riders.

- Popadom was an exception in more ways than one: he was the only coloured horse to win, the only one with a hogged mane and certainly the least aristocratic. Most of the leading horses have had a high percentage of thoroughbred blood. The Kingmaker, Barberry and Warrior were more or less pure-bred; Merely-a-Monarch's granddam was a Fell pony and his sire was Happy Monarch; and Doublet was out of an Argentinian polo pony by the steeplechasing sire Doubtless. Larkspur and Irish Cap both came from Ireland, though their ancestry is unknown; and Shaitan and M'Lord Connolly were part-bred Arabs.

- Maid Marion is the only mare to have won. Gretna Green, also ridden by Mark Phillips, Rise and Shine (Marietta Speed) and Granj from the Russian team in 1962 are the only ones to have come second.

Merely-a-Monarch is the only six-year-old to have headed the line-up, and Carawich and M'Lord Connolly the only seven-year-olds. George at eleven and St Finbarr at twelve are the veterans among the winners.

Burghley has never been won by a grey. Eight of the seventeen winners were bays, five were browns, three were chestnuts and Popadom was skewbald.

On five occasions Burghley has been won from the front: Merely-a-Monarch, Chalan, Don Camillo, Popadom and Doublet all established their ascendancy in the dressage and were never headed. The lowest dressage position from which the competition has been won is Warrior's 13th, although the marks were close that year. In 1972 Larkspur came up from 11th after the dressage.

Time on the cross-country has always been an important factor. Larkspur, Victoria Bridge and Shaitan were the fastest in the years in which they won, and M'Lord Connolly, Barberry and St Finbarr all gained maximum bonus. M'Lord Connolly is the only horse to have won in spite of a refusal on the cross-country.

Most of the winners have had clear rounds in the show jumping: though Chalan, Don Camillo, Maid Marion and Carawich all had one fence down, and Shaitan was lucky to keep his position with two down.

For a number of riders the show jumping has been where they have lost the competition. Jane Wykeham-Musgrave and Ryebrooks, Shelagh Kesler and Lochinvar, Toby Sturgis and Demi-Douzaine, David Goldie and Rembrandt and Karl Schultz and Madrigal would all be on the winners' roll if they had not made mistakes in the last phase.

Long acquaintanceship with the horse is clearly not an essential prerequisite for success. Judy Bradwell and Mark Phillips had both only ridden their mounts for a short time before the competition, as had Lucinda Prior-Palmer when she was second on Killaire in 1976.

(Left) *Karl Schultz and Madrigal, who in 1977 performed one of the best dressage tests ever seen at Burghley but suffered a dramatic reversal of fortune on the final day.*

(Right) *Lochinvar and Major Derek Allhusen in 1964. In his six appearances at Burghley, Lochinvar twice came near to winning.*

- The widest margin by which the competition has been won is Victoria Bridge's 57·6 in 1965. Merely-a-Monarch was nearly 34 points ahead of his nearest rival, and Doublet was 38.

- Richard Meade's appearances at Burghley cover the longest time span. His first was in 1961, when his horse Ad Astra broke down on the steeplechase. On Barberry he won in 1964 and was 2nd in 1966; in 1971 he was 5th on The Poacher; he was 5th in 1972 and 7th in 1974 on Wayfarer; and in 1975 he was 3rd on Tommy Buck.

- Both Mark Phillips and Jane Holderness-Roddam had their first outings at Burghley during the Pony Club Inter-Branch Championships in 1963 when they were members of the Beaufort team. Both have since performed consistently well here; Mark Phillips was 4th in 1967 on Rock On, 6th in 1971 on Great Ovation; he won in 1973, and was 2nd on Gretna Green in 1975. In 1974 he came near to winning when Columbus went lame, and in 1976 he would have won easily on Persian Holiday but for an unlucky fall at the Coffin. Jane Holderness-Roddam was 3rd in 1967, and again in 1968 on Our Nobby; on Warrior she won in 1976, and was 7th in 1977.

- The horse with the most consistent record at Burghley is Larkspur. In four appearances he and Janet Hodgson have finished no lower than 7th (in 1971). In 1970 he was 4th, in 1972 he won and in 1974 he was 4th again.

- Lochinvar competed on six occasions and twice came near to winning. In 1963, when ridden by Shelagh Kesler, he was in the lead after the cross-country but dropped to 2nd with 10 show jumping penalties. In 1968, ridden by his owner Derek Allhusen, he was again in the lead after the cross-country but was lame that evening and, with Mexico in mind, was withdrawn before the show jumping. In 1964 he was 4th after the second day, only to drop to 14th with a fall in the show jumping. In 1967 he was 5th, and in 1969 when on the short list for the European Championships, he completed only part of the competition. The only occasion on which he incurred any cross-country jumping penalties was 1966 when he took exception to the Spray Fence and deposited Derek Allhusen in the ditch.

- Smokey has the distinction of having clocked the fastest time on the cross-country on no less than three occasions—in 1970, 1973 and 1977, but his record was marred by falls in 1971 and 1974.

- Sioux ridden by Horst Karsten from Germany is the most familiar of the foreign horses. In three visits to Burghley he has been 6th (in 1972), unplaced (1974), and, in his best performance, 3rd (1977) at the age of 14.

- It seems to have been an advantage to have been last—or almost last—to go, for Merely-a-Monarch, Carawich and George were all last in the line-up, and Popadom was almost last. Warrior accomplished the unusual feat of winning from the position of having been first round the course. Grist to the mill of the superstitious is the fact that only once has number thirteen done well—Marietta Speed was number thirteen when she was 2nd in 1965—and on almost every other occasion it has been nearer the bottom than the top.

Results

1961

| | FIRST DAY | | SECOND DAY | | | | | | THIRD DAY | |
| | DRESSAGE | | STEEPLECHASE | | CROSS-COUNTRY | | END OF TWO DAYS | | SHOW JUMPING | FINAL SCORE |
	penalties	place	jumping penalties	time penalties	jumping penalties	time penalties	score	place	penalties	total points
1. Mrs. A. Gilroy's MERELY-A-MONARCH (Miss A. Drummond-Hay)	- 38	1st	—	+ 22.4	—	+ 46.4	+ 30.8	1st	—	+ 30.8
2. Lt. J. D. Smith-Bingham's BY GOLLY (owner)	- 79.33	4th	—	+ 37.6	—	+ 48.8	+ 7.07	2nd	- 10	- 2.93
3. Lt. The Hon. P. T. Conolly-Carew's BALLYHOO (owner)	- 107.33	11th	—	+ 22.4	- 20	+ 29.6	- 75.33	3rd	—	- 75.33
4. N. W. Gardiner's YOUNG PRETENDER (Lt.-Col. F. W. C. Weldon)	- 134.67	15th	—	+ 37.6	- 60	+ 59.6	- 97.47	4th	—	- 97.47
5. Captain and Mrs. J. J. Beale's ANONYMOUS (Capt. J. J. Beale)	96	8th	—	+ 37.6	- 60	+ 3.2	- 115.2	5th	- 10	- 125.2
6. Miss G. Tilney's LEANDER (owner)	- 128.67	14th	—	+ 37.6	- 100	+ 6	- 185.07	6th	- 10	- 195.07
7. Miss J. Sansome's NUTMEG (owner)	- 120.67	12th	—	+ 23.2	- 80	- 118.8	- 296.27	7th	—	- 296.27
8. OC The King's Troop RHA's SAVERNAKE (Capt. W. A. Dickins)	- 142	16th	—	+ 19.2	- 240	- 52.8	- 415.6	8th	- 20	- 435.6
9. Miss J. Sebag-Montefiore's SAMANTHA	- 125.33	13th	—	+ 32	- 420	- 52.4	- 565.73	9th	—	- 565.73

1962

TEAM RESULTS

1. USSR +2.2

Granj	+34.1
Satrap	- 12.7
Khirurg	- 19.2
(Rumb Withdrawn)	

2. IRELAND 93.3

St. Finbarr	+3.4
Sam Weller	- 35.4
Ballyhoo	- 61.3
(Irish Lace	- 184.1)

3. GREAT BRITAIN 160.2

Young Pretender	- 23.9
Sea Breeze	- 43.4
The Gladiator	- 92.9
(Mr. Wilson E)	

	FIRST DAY		SECOND DAY						THIRD DAY	
	DRESSAGE		STEEPLECHASE		CROSS-COUNTRY		END OF TWO DAYS		SHOW JUMPING	FINAL SCORE
	penalties	place	jumping penalties	time penalties	jumping penalties	time penalties	score	place	penalties	total points
1. Captain J. R. Templer's M'LORD CONNOLLY (owner)	- 60.5	4th	—	+37.6	- 20	+86	+43.1	2nd	—	+43.1
2. USSR Equestrian Federation's GRANJ (G. Gazjumov) (USSR)	- 89.5	17th	—	+37.6	—	+86	+34.1	3rd	—	+34.1
3. Miss J. Wykeham-Musgrave's RYEBROOKS (owner)	- 65.5	6th	—	+37.6	—	+78.8	+50.9	1st	- 20	+30.9
4. Capt. H. Freeman-Jackson's ST. FINBARR (owner)	- 79	14th	—	+33.6	—	+48.8	+3.4	6th	—	+3.4
5. USSR Equestrian Federation's SATRAP (P. Deev) (USSR)	- 61.5	5th	—	+35.2	- 20	+63.6	+17.3	4th	- 30	- 12.7
6. Mme. Le Roy's GARDEN (J. Le Roy) (France)	- 58.5	3rd	—	+29.6	- 20	+46	- 2.9	7th	- 10	- 12.9
7. USSR Equestrian Federation's KHIRURG (L. Baklyshkin) (USSR)	- 82	15th	—	+19.2	—	+73.6	+10.8	5th	- 30	- 19.2
8. N. W. Gardiner's YOUNG PRETENDER (Lt.-Col. F. W. C. Weldon)	- 113.5	25th	—	+36.8	—	+62.8	- 13.9	10th	- 10	- 23.9
9. A. Le Goupil's JACASSE B (owner) (France)	- 70	8th	—	+36	- 20	+40.8	- 13.2	9th	- 20	- 33.2
10. C. C. Cameron's SAM WELLER (A. Cameron) (Ireland)	- 107	24th	—	34.4	—	+57.2	- 15.4	11th	- 20	- 35.4
11. Col. V. D. S. Williams' SEA BREEZE (M. Bullen)	- 67	7th	—	+37.6	- 60	+86	- 3.4	8th	- 40	- 43.4
12. Miss B Pearson's ANNA'S BANNER (owner)	- 87	16th	—	+23.2	- 20	+28	- 45.8	12th	—	- 45.8

1963

	FIRST DAY		SECOND DAY						THIRD DAY	
	DRESSAGE		STEEPLECHASE		CROSS-COUNTRY		END OF TWO DAYS		SHOW JUMPING	FINAL SCORE
	penalties	place	jumping penalties	time penalties	jumping penalties	time penalties	score	place	penalties	total points
1. Capt. H. Freeman-Jackson's ST. FINBARR (owner) (Ireland)	- 63.33	5th	—	+37.6	—	+80.8	+55.07	3rd	—	+55.07
2. Maj. D. Allhusen's LOCHINVAR (Miss S. Kesler)	- 63	=3rd	—	+37.6	—	+80.8	+55.4	1st	- 10	+45.4
3. Centre National des Sports Equestres Militaires' LAURIER (Adj. J. Le Goff) (France)	- 63	=3rd	—	+37.6	—	+80.8	+55.4	2nd	- 10	+45.4
4. Mr. and Mrs. A. Kitchin's CHAR'S CHOICE (L. Sederholm)	- 62.67	2nd	—	+37.6	—	+62.8	+37.73	5th	—	+37.73
5. The King's Troop RHA's MASTER BERNARD (Sgt. R. S. Jones)	- 83.33	12th	—	+37.6	—	+80.8	+35.07	7th	- 10	+25.07
6. Capt. M. Whiteley's HAPPY TALK (owner)	- 89.33	15th	—	+28	—	+75.6	+14.27	12th	—	+14.27
7. M. Gabe's ICELUY (Capt. Landon) (France)	- 99.67	23rd	—	+37.6	—	+80.8	+18.73	9th	- 10	+8.73
8. C. C. Cameron's SAM WELLER (A. Cameron) (Ireland)	- 83.33	12th	—	+37.6	- 20	+80.8	+15.07	11th	- 10	+5.07
9. R. J. H. Meade's BARBERRY (owner)	- 86.33	14th	—	+37.6	—	+80.8	+32.07	8th	- 30	+2.07
10. Centre National des Sports Equestres Militaires' MICROBE (Lt. de Croutte) (France)	- 56.67	1st	—	+37.6	- 20	+48	+8.93	14th	- 10	- 1.07
11. The King's Troop RHA's HOT SPOT (Sgt. E. Witts)	- 65.67	7th	—	+37.6	- 20	+65.6	+17.53	10th	- 20	- 2.47
12. Mrs. R. F. Orford's SUNNY JIM (Mrs. J. J. Beale)	- 77.33	11th	—	+37.6	—	+75.2	+35.47	6th	- 40	- 4.53

1964

	FIRST DAY DRESSAGE		SECOND DAY STEEPLECHASE		CROSS-COUNTRY		END OF TWO DAYS		THIRD DAY SHOW JUMPING	FINAL SCORE
	penalties	place	jumping penalties	time penalties	jumping penalties	time penalties	score	place	penalties	total points
•1. R. J. H. Meade's BARBERRY (owner)	- 45.5	6th	—	+ 31.2	—	+ 75.6	+ 61.3	1st	—	+ 61.3
2. J. Mehrdorf's ILTSCHI (owner) (W. Germany)	- 39.5	3rd	—	+ 20	—	+ 62.4	+ 42.9	3rd	—	+ 42.9
3. The King's Troop RHA's MASTER BERNARD (Sgt. R. S. Jones)	- 41.5	4th	*—	+ 31.2	—	+ 73.6	+ 45.3	2nd	- 10	+ 35.3*
4. Major E. A. Boylan's DURLAS EILE (owner) (Ireland)	- 64	9th	—	+ 25.6	—	+ 75.6	+ 37.2	5th	- 10	+ 27.2
5. L. Goessing's KING (owner) (W. Germany)	- 37.5	= 1st	*—	+ 30.4	- 20	+ 66.4	+ 23.3	6th	—	23.3f
6. Miss M. Macdonell's KILMACTHOMAS (owner)	- 82.5	19th	—	+ 27.2	—	+ 58.4	+ 3.1	7th	--	+ 3.1
7. Miss C. Sheppard's FENJIRAO (owner)	- 69	12th	—	+ 18.4	- 20	+ 70.8	+ 0.2	8th	—	+ 0.2
8. The King's Troop RHA's SIR FRANCIS (Capt. H. B. de Fonblanque)	- 106.5	26th	—	+ 30.4	—	+ 74.4	- 1.7	9th	- 10	- 11.7
9. H. Graham-Clark's FRENCH FROLIC (Miss J. Graham-Clark)	- 74	16th	—	+ 30.4	- 20	+ 50.4	- 13.2	10th	—	- 13.2
10. Mrs. S. Waddington's GLENAMOY (owner)	- 37.5	= 1st	—	+ 31.2	- 80	+ 58.8	- 27.5	13th	—	- 27.5
11. Miss E. Meynell's QUESTION GIRL (N. Simpson)	- 128.5	34th	—	+ 31.2	—	+ 74	- 23.3	12th	- 10	- 33.3
12. The Hon. W. R. Leigh's MARSHALL TUDOR (owner)	- 101	24th	—	+ 31.2	- 20	+ 75.6	- 14.2	11th	- 20	- 34.2

* Includes 18 penalties on Phase C
f Includes 16 penalties on Phase C

1965

	FIRST DAY DRESSAGE		SECOND DAY STEEPLECHASE		CROSS-COUNTRY		END OF TWO DAYS		THIRD DAY SHOW JUMPING	FINAL SCORE
	penalties	place	jumping penalties	time penalties	jumping penalties	time penalties	score	place	penalties	total points
1. Capt. and Mrs. J. J. Beale's VICTORIA BRIDGE (Capt. J. J. Beale)	- 61.9	2nd	—	+ 36.8	—	+ 67.2	+ 42.1	1st	—	+ 42.1
2. Miss M. Speed's RISE AND SHINE (owner)	- 91.9	14th	—	+ 37.6	—	+ 62.8	+ 4.5	2nd	- 20	- 15.5*
3. Miss J. Walkington's MERRY JUDGE (owner)	- 92.5	15th	—	+ 18.4	—	+ 32	- 42.1	8th	—	- 42.1
4. H. Graham-Clark's PRIAM (Miss J. Graham-Clark)	- 86.5	12th	—	+ 25.6	—	+ 33.2	- 27.7	3rd	- 20	- 47.7
5. The Hon. Mrs. Hely-Hutchinson's COUNT JASPER (Miss P. Hely-Hutchinson)	- 75	5th	—	+ 18.4	—	+ 18.8	- 37.8	6th	- 10	- 47.8
6. Miss P. J. Cawston's CHARM (owner)	- 99.4	18th	—	+ 4.8	—	+ 60.4	- 34.2	4th	- 20	- 54.2
7. H. Graham-Clark's FRENCH FROLIC (Miss J. Graham-Clark)	- 79	7th	—	+ 24.8	- 20	+ 38.8	- 35.4	5th	- 20	- 55.4
8. Miss B. Pearson's EASTER BOUQUET (owner)	- 85.5	11th	—	+ 28.8	- 40	+ 26.8	- 69.9	11th	—	- 69.9
9. Capt. H. Freeman-Jackson's MERCURY (A. Lillingston)	- 83.5	9th	—	+ 30.4	- 60	+ 52.4	- 60.7	9th	- 10	- 70.7
10. Mrs. T. W. Kopanski's THE LITTLE MERMAID (owner)	- 73.5	3rd	—	+ 2.4	—	+ 32	- 39.1	7th	- 40.5	- 79.6
11. M. Tucker's THE VIKING (owner)	- 114	27th	—	+ 11.2	—	+ 32	- 70.8	12th	- 10	- 80.8
12. Miss F. Pearson's TAM O'TULLOCHAN (owner)	- 102.4	21st	—	+ 37.6	- 60	+ 40.8	- 84	14th	—	- 84

*Includes 4 penalties on Phase C

117

1966

| | FIRST DAY | | SECOND DAY | | | | | | THIRD DAY | |
| | DRESSAGE | | STEEPLECHASE | | CROSS-COUNTRY | | END OF TWO DAYS | | SHOW JUMPING | FINAL SCORE |
	penalties	place	jumping penalties	time penalties	jumping penalties	time penalties	score	place	penalties	total points
1. Capt. C. Moratorio's CHALAN (owner) (Argentina)	- 42.5	1st	—	+ 37.6	—	+ 78	+ 73.1	1st	- 10	+ 63.1
2. R. J. H. Meade's BARBERRY (owner)	- 77	20th	—	+ 37.6	—	- 86	+ 46.6	4th	—	+ 46.6
3. Miss V. Freeman-Jackson's SAM WELLER (owner) (Ireland)	- 62	11th	—	+ 37.6	—	+ 86	+ 61.6	2nd	- 20	+ 41.6
4. Major E. A. Boylan's DURLAS EILE (owner) (Ireland)	- 54	6th	—	+ 37.6	—	+ 67.6	+ 51.2	3rd	- 10	+ 41.2
5. M. Whiteley's THE POACHER (owner)	- 68.5	13th	—	+ 37.6	—	+ 64	+ 33.1	5th	—	+ 33.1
6. USSR Equestrian Federation's PAKET (P. Deev) (USSR)	- 55	7th	—	+ 37.6	- 20	+ 60.8	+ 23.4	8th	—	+ 23.4
7. Miss C. Sheppard's FENJIRAO (owner)	- 58	8th	—	+ 37.6	—	+ 53.2	+ 32.8	6th	- 10	+ 22.8
8. Sir John Galvin's LOUGHLIN (Miss P. Moreton) (Ireland)	- 86	28th	—	+ 37.6	—	+ 46	- 2.4	10th	—	- 2.4
9. Mrs. C. D. Plumb's M'LORD CONNOLLY (K. Freeman) (USA)	- 71	16th	—	+ 37.6	- 60	+ 82.4	- 11	12th	—	- 11
10. T. Durston-Smith's DREAMY DASHER (owner)	- 107.5	36th	—	+ 37.6	—	+ 74	+ 4.1	9th	- 20	- 15.9
11. Sub.-Lt. E. C. Atkinson's PRIAM (owner)	- 70	15th	—	+ 37.6	- 60	+ 83.6	- 8.8	11th	- 10	- 18.8
12. Mrs. A. B. Whiteley's FOXDOR (Mrs. A. Oliver)	- 75	20th		+ 37.6	- 60	+ 66.8	- 30.6	13th	- 10	- 40.6

1967

| | FIRST DAY | | SECOND DAY | | | | | | THIRD DAY | |
| | DRESSAGE | | STEEPLECHASE | | CROSS-COUNTRY | | END OF TWO DAYS | | SHOW JUMPING | FINAL SCORE |
	penalties	place	jumping penalties	time penalties	jumping penalties	time penalties	score	place	penalties	total points
1. Miss L. Sutherland's POPADOM (owner)	- 28	1st	—	+ 37.6	—	+ 61.2	+ 70.8	1st	—	+ 70.8
2. Miss A. Roger Smith's QUESTIONNAIRE (owner)	- 51.67	6th	—	+ 36.8	—	+ 75.6	+ 60.73	2nd	—	+ 60.73
3. Miss J. Bullen's OUR NOBBY (owner)	- 58.67	15th	—	+ 28.8	—	+ 72	+ 42.13	8th	—	+ 42.13
4. M. Phillips' ROCK ON (owner)	- 76.33	36th	—	+ 37.6	—	+ 75.6	+ 36.87	10th	—	+ 36.87
5. Major D. S. Allhusen's LOCHINVAR (owner)	- 51.33	5th	—	+ 37.6	—	+ 69.6	+ 55.87	4th	- 20	+ 35.87
6. Mr. & Mrs. A. Kitchin's CHAR'S CHOICE (P. Welch)	- 66.67	24th	—	+ 37.6	—	+ 64	+ 34.93	11th	—	+ 34.93
7. W. Haggard's CHALAN (owner) (USA)	- 50	4th	—	+ 37.6	—	+ 63.2	+ 50.8	5th	- 20	+ 30.8
8. Miss S. Lord's EVENING MAIL (owner) (USA)	- 65.67	22nd	—	+ 37.6	—	+ 75.6	+ 47.53	7th	- 20	+ 27.53
9. Miss J. Jobling-Purser's JENNY (owner)	- 48.33	3rd	—	+ 36.8	—	+ 41.2	+ 29.67	12th	- 10	+ 19.67
10. J. Shedden's HEYDAY (Mrs. S. Waddington)	- 54.33	8th	—	+ 37.6	—	+ 64.8	+ 48.07	6th	- 30	+ 18.07
11. M. Herbert's ARGONAUT (owner)	- 54.67	9th	—	+ 37.6	—	+ 54.8	+ 37.73	9th	- 20	+ 17.73
12. Miss M. Macdonell's KILMACTHOMAS (owner)	- 67.67	24th	—	+ 37.6	'—	+ 56.4	+ 26.33	13th	- 10	+ 16.31

	FIRST DAY DRESSAGE		SECOND DAY STEEPLECHASE		SECOND DAY CROSS-COUNTRY		SECOND DAY END OF TWO DAYS		THIRD DAY SHOW JUMPING	THIRD DAY FINAL SCORE
	penalties	place	jumping penalties	time penalties	jumping penalties	time penalties	score	place	penalties	total points
1. Miss S. Willcox's FAIR AND SQUARE (owner)	- 39.17	3rd	—	+ 37.6	—	+ 28.8	+ 27.23	2nd	- .5	+ 26.73
2. Miss S. Neill's PERI (owner)	- 69.33	26th	—	+ 37.6	—	+ 51.6	+ 19.87	3rd	- 10	+ 9.87
3. Miss J. Bullen's OUR NOBBY (owner)	- 78.33	33rd	—	+ 37.6	—	+ 48.4	+ 7.67	5th	—	+ 7.67
4. H. Michel's OURAGAN C (owner) (France)	- 48.67	=4th	—	+ 37.6	—	+ 28	+ 16.93	4th	- 20	- 3.07
5. O. Vaughan-Jones' ALL OVER (owner)	- 76	32nd	—	+ 36	—	+ 44	+ 4	6th	- 10	- 6
6. Executors late N. P. Gold's SHAITAN (Miss G. Watson)	- 73	30th	—	+ 32	—	+ 23.6	- 17.4	8th	—	- 17.4
7. Mrs. C. M. Parker's CORNISHMAN (S/Sgt. R. S. Jones)	- 55.33	7th	—	+ 37.6	- 20	+ 28	- 9.73	7th	—	- 29.73
8. Brig. M. Gordon-Watson's CORNISHMAN V (S/Sgt. R S Jones)	- 55.33	7th	—	+ 37.6	- 20	+ 28	- 9.73	7th	—	- 29.73
9. Mrs. C. M. Parker's MANX MONARCH (owner)	- 66.33	17th	—	+ 29.6	- 80	+ 48	- 68.73	13th	—	- 68.73
10. Miss C. Lockhart's GAMECOCK (owner)	- 67.67	20th	—	+ 18.4	- 20	- .4	- 69.67	14th	- 10	- 79.67
11. M. Whiteley's THE POACHER (owner)	- 68	21st	—	+ 28	- 60	+ 22.4	- 77.6	15th	- 20	- 97.6
12. Mrs. C. Horton's THE DARK HORSE (owner)	- 64.67	16th	—	- 4	- 20	- 3.6	- 92.27	17th	- 20	- 112.27

	FIRST DAY DRESSAGE		SECOND DAY STEEPLECHASE		SECOND DAY CROSS-COUNTRY		SECOND DAY END OF TWO DAYS		THIRD DAY SHOW JUMPING	THIRD DAY FINAL SCORE
	penalties	place	jumping penalties	time penalties	jumping penalties	time penalties	score	place	penalties	total points
1. Mrs. M. Stinton's and Mr., Mrs. and Miss Smallwood's SHAITAN (Miss G. Watson)	- 57.33	3rd	—	+ 37.6	—	+ 73.6	+ 53.87	1st	- 20	+ 33.87
2. Mrs. M. Laurent's SKYBORN (M. Tucker)	- 74.33	17th	—	+ 37.6	—	+ 72	+ 35.27	2nd	- 10	+ 25.27
3. Miss L. Sutherland's POPADOM (owner)	- 53.33	1st	—	+ 34.4	—	+ 34.8	+ 15.87	4th	—	+ 15.87
4. Miss S. Neill's PERI (owner)	- 74.67	18th	—	+ 37.6	- 20	+ 69.2	+ 12.13	5th	—	+ 12.13
5. Lt.-Col. M. A. Q. Darley's CORNCRAKE (owner)	- 61.67	7th	—	+ 37.6	—	+ 45.6	+ 21.53	3rd	- 10	+ 11.53
6. Mrs. H. Wilkin's SEA QUEST (M. Bullen)	- 72.67	15th	—	+ 37.6	- 20	+ 55.6	+ .53	8th	- 10	- 9.47
7. Miss T. Martin-Bird's SPIRIDION (owner)	- 65.67	9th	—	+ 37.6	- 20	+ 54.8	+ 6.73	7th	- 20	- 13.27
8. T. R. Sturgis's COCO (owner)	- 98.33	31st	—	+ 37.6	- 20	+ 67.2	- 13.53	9th	—	- 13.53
9. Miss L. Sutherland's GYPSY FLAME (owner)	- 56.67	2nd	—	+ 37.6	- 60	+ 61.6	- 17.47	10th	—	- 17.47
10. Lt. E. C. Atkinson's MAGIC CARPET (owner)	- 75.33	20th	—	+ 37.6	—	+ 69.6	+ 11.87	6th	- 30	- 18.13
11. T. Durston-Smith's HENRY THE NAVIGATOR (owner)	- 72	14th	—	+ 20.8	- 20	+ 40.4	- 30.8	14th	—	- 30.8
12. Capt. and Mrs. C. Kendall's PJ-LL ESQ (J. Smart)	- 71.33	13th	- 60	+ 37.6	—	+ 72	- 21.73	11th	- 10	- 31.73

	FIRST DAY DRESSAGE		SECOND DAY STEEPLECHASE		CROSS-COUNTRY		END OF TWO DAYS		THIRD DAY SHOW JUMPING	FINAL SCORE
	penalties	place	jumping penalties	time penalties	jumping penalties	time penalties	score	place	penalties	total points
1. R. Smith's DON CAMILLO (Miss J. Bradwell)	- 28.67	1st	—	+ 37.6	—	+ 54.8	+ 63.73	2nd	- 10	+ 53.73
2. Mr. and Mrs. Compton-Bracebridge's UPPPER STRATA (R.D. Walker)	- 53.67	13th	—	+ 37.6	—	+ 61.6	+ 45.53	4th	—	+ 45.53
3. W. Goldie's REMBRANDT (D. Goldie)	- 42.67	3rd	—	+ 37.6	—	+ 68.8	+ 63.73	1st	- 20	+ 43.73
4. Miss J. Hodgson's LARKSPUR (owner)	- 52	11th	—	+ 37.6	—	+ 63.6	+ 49.2	3rd	- 10	+ 39.2
5. Miss D. West's BACCARAT (owner)	- 69	27th	—	+ 37.6	—	+ 72	+ 40.6	5th	- 10	+ 30.6
6. Miss A. Sowden's MOONCOIN (owner)	- 58.67	16th	—	+ 37.6	—	+ 50.4	+ 29.33	7th	—	+ 29.33
7. M. Moffett's DEMERARA (owner)	- 53	12th	—	+ 37.6	—	+ 38	+ 22.6	8th	—	+ 22.6
8. Miss J. Neill's PERI (Miss S. Neill)	- 65	21st	—	+ 37.6	—	+ 59.6	+ 32.2	6th	- 10	+ 22.2
9. W. Powell-Harris's SMOKEY (owner) (Ireland)	- 92	32nd	—	+ 36	—	+ 75.6	+ 19.6	9th	—	+ 19.6
10. J. B. Eastwood's SLIEVE NAMON (Miss A. Fenwick)	- 72	28th	—	+ 32.8	- 20	+ 49.6	- 9.6	15th	—	- 9.6
11. Mrs. A. Franks' SAM (Miss B. Chambers)	- 54.67	14th	—	+ 37.6	- 60	+ 69.6	- 7.47	14th	- 10	- 17.47
12. Miss F. Lochore's THE YOUNG LAIRD (owner)	- 49	9th	—	+ 28	—	+ 29.6	+ 8.6	10th	- 30	- 21.4

TEAM RESULTS

1. GREAT BRITAIN - 333.3
   Baccarat — - 98.1
   Cornishman V — - 117
   The Poacher — - 118.2
   (Great Ovation — - 126.9)

2. USSR - 755.5
   Resfeder — - 160.6
   Obzor — - 262.6
   Farkhad — - 332.3
   (Rashod Eliminated)

3. IRELAND - 795.6
   Ballangarry — - 193
   Broken Promise — - 290.6
   Smokey VI — - 312
   (San Carlos Withdrawn)

	FIRST DAY DRESSAGE		SECOND DAY STEEPLECHASE		CROSS-COUNTRY		END OF TWO DAYS		THIRD DAY SHOW JUMPING	FINAL SCORE
	penalties	place	jumping penalties	time penalties	jumping penalties	time penalties	score	place	penalties	total points
1. HRH the Princess Anne's DOUBLET (owner)	- 41.5	1st	—	—	—	- 18.8	- 60.3	1st	—	- 60.3
2. Miss D. West's BACCARAT (owner)	- 62.5	10th	—	—	—	- 25.6	- 88.1	2nd	- 10	- 98.1
3. The Hon. Mrs. F. Westenra's CLASSIC CHIPS (S. Stevens)	- 98.5	35th	—	—	—	- 4.4	- 102.9	4th	- 10	- 112.9
4. Brig. M. Gordon-Watson's CORNISHMAN V (Miss M. Gordon-Watson)	- 71	15th	—	—	—	- 26	- 97	3rd	- 20	- 117
5. The Combined Training Committee's THE POACHER (R. J. H. Meade)	- 59	6th	—	—	- 20	- 29.2	- 108.2	5th	- 10	- 118.2
6. Miss F. and Lt. M. Phillips' GREAT OVATION (Lt. M. Phillips)	- 64.5	12th	—	—	- 20	- 32.4	- 116.9	7th	- 10	- 126.9
7. Miss J. Hodgson's LARKSPUR (owner)	- 84.5	23rd	—	—	—	- 31.2	- 115.7	6th	- 20	- 135.7
8. Miss A. Sowden's MOONCOIN (owner)	- 84	22nd	—	—	—	- 52	- 136	8th	—	- 136
9. Col. H. Buehler's WUKARI (1st Lt. A. Buehler) (Switz)	- 73.5	17th	—	- 18.4	—	- 52	- 143.9	9th	—	- 143.9
10. USSR Equestrian Federation's RESFEDER (Mr. Muhin) (USSR)	- 49	2nd	—	- .8	- 80	- 30.8	- 160.6	10th	—	- 160.6
11. Swedish Army's SARAJEVO (J. Jonsson) (Sweden)	- 59.5	8th	- 60	—	—	- 55.6	- 175.1	12th	—	- 175.1
12. T. Durston-Smith's and Miss M. Rock's HENRY THE NAVIGATOR (T.Durston-Smith)	- 85.5	25th	—	—	- 60	- 39.6	- 185.1	14th	—	- 185.1

| | FIRST DAY | | SECOND DAY | | | | | | THIRD DAY | |
| | DRESSAGE | | STEEPLECHASE | | CROSS COUNTRY | | END OF TWO DAYS | | SHOW JUMPING | FINAL SCORE |
	penalties	place	jumping penalties	time penalties	jumping penalties	time penalties	score	place	penalties	total points
1. Miss J. Hodgson's LARKSPUR (owner)	- 47	=11th	—	—	—	- 8	- 55	1st	—	- 55
2. Miss D. West's BACCARAT (owner)	- 48	13th	—	—	—	- 10	- 58	2nd	—	- 58
3. Mrs. D. Brentnall's MARY POPPINS II (Miss H. Booth)	- 43	7th	—	—	—	- 16.4	- 59.4	3rd	—	- 59.4
4. Miss L. Prior-Palmer's BE FAIR (owner)	- 47	=11th	—	- 2.4	—	- 10.4	- 59.8	4th	—	- 59.8
5. Mrs. H. Wilkin's WAYFARER II (R. J. H. Meade)	- 38	4th	—	—	—	- 24.4	- 62.4	5th	- 10	- 72.4
6. W. Baldus' SIOUX (H. Karsten) (W. Germany)	- 38.67	5th	—	—	—	- 56	- 94.67	9th	—	- 94.67
7. The Hon. Mrs. F. Westenra's CLASSIC CHIPS (S. Stevens)	- 58	17th	—	—	20	- 21.6	- 94.6	8th	- 10	- 104.6
8. Mr. and Mrs. M. Tucker's MOONCOIN (Mrs. M. Tucker)	- 59	21st	—	—	—	- 46	- 105	10th	—	- 105
9. Lt.-Col and Mrs. C. and Miss A. Sivewright's ALSEDELL (Miss A. Sivewright)	- 66.33	29th	—	—	—	- 39.6	- 105.93	-11th	—	- 105.93
10. Miss L. Sutherland's PEER GYNT (owner)	- 27.33	1st	—	—	40	- 43.6	- 110.93	12th	—	- 110.93
11. Miss E. Profumo's WESTERN MORN (Miss J. Bullen)	- 71	31st	—	- .8	—	- 41.2	- 113	13th	- 10	- 123
12. Miss A. L. C. Daybell's WITCH GIRL (J. Marsden)	- 85	58th	—	- 16.8	—	- 37.2	- 139	18th	—	- 139

| | FIRST DAY | | SECOND DAY | | | | | | THIRD DAY | |
| | DRESSAGE | | STEEPLECHASE | | CROSS-COUNTRY | | END OF TWO DAYS | | SHOW JUMPING | FINAL SCORE |
	penalties	place	jumping penalties	time penalties	jumping penalties	time penalties	score	place	penalties	total points
1. A. E. and A. G. Hill's MAID MARION (Captain M. Phillips)	- 41.57	2nd	—	—	—	- 15.6	- 57.27	1st	- 10	- 67.27
2. Mrs. M. J. and Miss D. Thorne's THE KINGMAKER (Miss D. Thorne)	- 71.33	29th	—	—	—	- 5.2	- 76.53	3rd	—	- 76.53
3. Mrs. A. H. and Miss S. Hatherly's HARLEY (Miss S. Hatherly)	-62.67	14th	—	—	—	- 8.4	- 71.07	2nd	- 10	- 81.07
4. C. Collins' CENTURIAN (owner)	- 54.33	4th	—	- 8	—	- 24.4	- 86.73	6th	—	- 86.73
5. Miss L. Sutherland's PEER GYNT (owner)	- 47.33	3rd	—	- 3.2	- 20	- 27.6	- 98.13	9th	—	- 98.13
6. Mrs. and Miss J. Starkey's ACROBAT (Miss J. Starkey)	- 75	33rd	—	—	—	- 24.8	- 99.8	10th	—	- 99.8
7. C. Wares' GAVELACRE (owner)	- 64.67	18th	—	—	—	- 36	- 100.67	12th	—	- 100.67
8. W. Powell-Harris's SMOKEY VI (owner) (Ireland)	- 81.33	39th	—	—	—	—	- 81.33	5th	- 21	- 102.33
9. Miss J. Crossland's TOUCH AND GO III (Miss M. Frank)	- 65.33	19th	—	—	—	- 28	- 93.33	8th	- 20	- 113.33
10. Mr. and Mrs. T. R. Sturgis' DEMI-DOUZAINE (T. R. Sturgis)	- 79.67	36th	—	- 5.6	—	- 15.2	- 100.47	11th	- 21	- 121.47
11. Miss K. Hill's DAY RETURN (owner)	- 67.33	24th	—	—	—	- 10	- 77.33	4th	- 44.25	- 121.58
12. M. Moffett's DEMERARA (owner)	- 75	32nd	—	—	- 20	- 8	- 103	13th	- 20	- 123

1974

	FIRST DAY DRESSAGE		SECOND DAY STEEPLECHASE		SECOND DAY CROSS-COUNTRY		END OF TWO DAYS		THIRD DAY SHOW JUMPING	THIRD DAY FINAL SCORE
	penalties	place	jumping penalties	time penalties	jumping penalties	time penalties	score	place	penalties	total points
1. B. O. Davidson's IRISH CAP (owner) (USA)	- 45.67	2nd	—	—	—	- 26	- 71.67	2nd	—	- 71.67
2. U.S. Equestrian Team's GOOD MIXTURE (J. M. Plumb) (USA)	- 58.33	= 16th	—	—	—	- 13.6	- 71.93	3rd	—	- 71.93
3. H. Thomas's PLAYMAR (owner)	- 59.67	21st	—	—	—	- 12.8	- 72.47	4th	—	- 72.47
4. Miss J. Hodgson's LARKSPUR (owner)	- 54.67	8th	—	- 4	—	- 30.8	- 89.47	5th	—	- 89.47
5. Minister for Defence's BOTHAR BUI (Capt. R. MacMahon) (Ireland)	- 72.67	50th	—	—	—	- 26.4	- 99.07	7th	—	- 99.07
6. R. Perkins' FURTIVE (Miss E. T. Perkins) (USA)	- 50.3	35th	—	—	—	- 46.4	- 96.73	6th	- 10	- 106.73
7. Mrs. H. Wilkin's WAYFARER II (R. J. H. Meade)	- 58.33	= 16th	--	- 9.6	—	- 47.2	- 115.13	11th	—	- 115.13
8. Mr. and Mrs. E. B. Graham's SUMATRA (Miss J. Graham) (Canada)	- 74.67	53rd	—	—	—	- 47.6	- 122.27	12th	- .75	- 123.02
9. Mrs. C. M. Parker's CORNISH GOLD (owner)	- 63.67	31st	—	—	- 20	- 29.6	- 113.27	9th	- 10	- 123.27
10. Miss L. Prior-Palmer's BE FAIR (owner)	- 66	39th	—	- 28	—	- 33.6	- 127.6	13th	—	- 127.6
11. Mr. and Mrs. T. R. Sturgis' DEMI-DOUZAINE (T. R. Sturgis)	- 70.67	46th	—	- 4	—	- 36.4	- 111.07	8th	- 20.5	- 131.57
12. HM the Queen's GOODWILL (HRH the Princess Anne, Mrs. M. Phillips)	- 69	42nd	—	- 4	- 20	- 45.6	- 138.6	15th	- .5	- 139.1

1975

	FIRST DAY DRESSAGE		SECOND DAY STEEPLECHASE		SECOND DAY CROSS-COUNTRY		END OF TWO DAYS		THIRD DAY SHOW JUMPING	THIRD DAY FINAL SCORE
	penalties	place	jumping penalties	time penalties	jumping penalties	time penalties	score	place	penalties	total points
1. A. Colquhoun's CARAWICH (Miss A. Pattinson)	- 54.67	7th	—	—	—	—	- 54.67	1st	- 10	- 64.67
2. Mrs. J. R. Hodgson's GRETNA GREEN (Captain M. Phillips)	- 64.33	15th	—	—	—	- 7.2	- 71.53	6th	—	- 71.53
3. M. D. Abrahams' TOMMY BUCK (R. J. H. Meade)	- 60.33	12th	—	- .8	—	- 2.4	- 63.53	2nd	- 10	- 73.53
4. Mr. and Mrs. R. D. S. Carpendale's FAVOUR (J. Kersley)	- 74.33	31st	—	—	—	—	- 74.33	7th	—	- 74.33
5. Mrs. R. B. Lunger's TOUCH AND GO (Miss M. Frank)	- 46.33	3rd	—	—	—	- 21.6	- 67.93	4th	- 10	- 77.93
6. Mrs. and Miss J. Starkey's ACROBAT (Miss J. Starkey)	- 70	28th	—	—	—	- 9.2	- 79.2	11th	—	- 79.2
7. Miss P. Biden's LITTLE EXTRA (owner)	- 69.67	27th	—	—	—	—	- 69.67	5th	- 10	- 79.67
8. The Viscountess Brookeborough's VILLAGE GOSSIP (Miss K. O'Hara)	- 66	19th	—	—	—	—	- 66	3rd	- 20	- 86
9. M. Moffett's DEMERARA (owner)	- 80.67	44th	—	—	—	—	- 80.67	12th	- 10	- 90.67
10. Miss D. Thorne's THE KINGMAKER (owner)	- 82	45th	—	—	—	—	- 82	13th	- 10	- 92
11. Mrs W. and Miss D. West's BENJIE (Miss D. West)	- 55	8th	—	—	- 20	- 8	- 83	14th	- 10	- 93
12. Mrs. P. Gormley's MASTER QUESTION (J. Seaman)	- 68.67	23rd	—	- 2.4	—	- 13.2	- 84.27	15th	- 10	- 94.27

	DRESSAGE (FIRST DAY)		STEEPLECHASE (SECOND DAY)		CROSS-COUNTRY		END OF TWO DAYS		SHOW JUMPING (THIRD DAY)	FINAL SCORE
	penalties	place	jumping penalties	time penalties	jumping penalties	time penalties	score	place	penalties	total points
1. Mrs. S. Howard's WARRIOR (Mrs. T. Holderness-Roddam)	- 67	13th	—	- 9.6	—	- 18.4	- 95	2nd	—	- 95
2. C. A. Cyzer's KILLAIRE (Miss L. Prior-Palmer)	- 68.33	15th	—	- 26.4	—	- 5.6	- 100.33	5th	—	- 100.33
3. Mr. and Mrs. G. Brookes' WELTON PLAYBOY (Miss S. Brookes)	- 66.33	11th	—	- 17.6	—	- 16	- 99.93	4th	- 10	- 109.93
4. Mrs. and Miss J. Starkey's TOPPER TOO (Miss J. Starkey)	- 59.67	6th	—	- 21.6	—	- 30.4	- 111.67	8th	—	- 111.67
5. Mr. and Mrs. T. R. Sturgis's DEMI-DOUZAINE (T. R. Sturgis)	- 74	25th	—	16	—	- 4	- 94	1st	- 20	- 114
6. Mrs. J. Geekie's COPPER TIGER (Miss C. Geekie)	- 61.33	8th	—	- 24.8	—	- 21.6	- 107.73	7th	- 10	- 117.73
7. Miss J. Thorne's SPARTAN BOY (owner)	- 76	31st	—	- 13.6	—	- 25.2	- 114.8	9th	- 10	- 124.8
8. Captain M. Phillips PERSIAN HOLIDAY (owner)	- 52	1st	—	- 8.8	60	- 6.4	- 127.2	12th	—	- 127.2
9. R. Clarke's ALOOF (Miss S. Hatherly)	- 89	50th	—	- 16	—	- 24	- 129	14th	—	- 129
10. N. Engert's MILLE TONNERRES (owner)	- 79	38th	—	- 16.8	—	- 27.2	- 123	10th	10	- 133
11. Miss P. M. Maher's BALLANGARRY (owner) (Ireland)	- 74.67	27th	—	- 32.8	—	- 38	- 145.47	21st	—	- 145.47
12. Miss E. Boone's FELDAY FARMER (owner)	- 87.67	48th	—	- 8.8	—	- 9.6	- 106.07	6th	- 40	- 146.07

	DRESSAGE (FIRST DAY)		STEEPLECHASE (SECOND DAY)		CROSS-COUNTRY		END OF TWO DAYS		SHOW JUMPING (THIRD DAY)	FINAL SCORE
	penalties	place	jumping penalties	time penalties	jumping penalties	time penalties	score	place	penalties	total points
1. Mrs. H. C. Straker's GEORGE (Miss L. Prior-Palmer)	31.75	3rd	—	—	—	- 5.6	- 37.35	2nd	—	- 37.35
2. Gestüt Nehmten's MADRIGAL (K. Schultz) (W. Germany)	- 21	1st	—	—	—	- 8	- 29	1st	- 10	- 39
3. Dr. Baldus and G. Weyhausen SIOUX (H. Karsten) (W. Germany)	- 35	7th	—	—	—	- 3.2	- 38.2	3rd	- 10	- 48.2
4. Mrs. M. J. and Miss D. Thorne's THE KINGMAKER (Miss D. Thorne)	- 47.5	23rd	—	—	—	- 4.8	- 52.3	5th	—	- 52.3
5. Mrs. T. Holderness-Roddam's WARRIOR (owner)	- 43.5	19th	—	—	—	- 10.4	- 53.9	6th	—	- 53.9
6. Major G. T. Ponsonby's CAMBRIDGE BLUE (J. Watson) (Ireland)	- 57.25	38th	—	—	—	- .8	- 58.05	8th	—	- 58.05
7. C. Collins' SMOKEY VI (owner)	- 40	16th	—	—	—	—	- 40	4th	- 20	- 60
8. Mme. A. Souchon BEGIUN CHARRIERE (A. Souchon) (France)	- 47	22nd	—	—	—	- 21.6	- 68.6	9th	—	- 68.6
9. USSR Equestrian Federation's BALADZHAR (M. Gubarev) (USSR)	- 48.75	28th	—	- 7.2	—	- 14.8	- 70.75	10th	—	- 70.75
10. A. Colquhoun's CARAWICH (Mrs. A. Adsetts)	- 34.75	6th	—	—	—	- 20.4	- 55.15	7th	- 20	- 75.15
11. C. F. Harrison's CHEAL CLOUD (Mrs. M. Comerford)	- 48.75	28th	—	—	—	- 22.8	- 71.55	11th	- 10	- 81.55
12. Mrs. and Miss J. Starkey's TOPPER TOO (Miss J. Starkey)	- 36	8th	—	—	—	- 46	- 82	14th	—	- 82

TEAM RESULTS

1. GREAT BRITAIN - 151.25
   - George — - 37.35
   - Smokey — - 60
   - Warrior — - 53.9
   - (Merry Sovereign W.)

2. GERMANY - 221.9
   - Madrigal — - 39
   - Sioux — - 48.2
   - Akzent — - 134.7
   - (El Paso Retired)

3. IRELAND - 247.9
   - Cambridge Blue — - 58.05
   - Pontoon — - 91.75
   - Ballangarry — - 98.1
   - (Blue Tom Tit Retired)

The Pony Club Horse Trials Championships

For three years, from 1963 until 1965, the Pony Club Horse Trials Championships were held at Burghley: the main action taking place on the day after the Three-Day Event. The Pony Club Championships were already well established, having been first held in 1949, and to win them was the ambition of many a Pony Club member.

It is typical of the spirit of enterprise and of 'nothing is impossible' that Lord Exeter and the Horse Trials organisation undertook such an additional burden. It was not the only one that they shouldered, for there has always been a wide variety of additional competitions at Burghley. In 1963, for example, there were also the Pony Club Team Jumping, the Zone Finals of the Pony Club mounted games, the Prince Philip Cup and the Regional Final of the Daily Express Foxhunter jumping competition—as well as the usual top grade show jumping.

The under-eighteen Pony Club teams from all over the country had competed earlier at Area Trials, and the winning teams and the individual winners contested the Championships at Burghley. There was also a Senior Championship for riders between eighteen and twenty who had won a separate competition in the Area Trials.

The story of the Championships at Burghley is really the story of the period of ascendancy of the West Norfolk Hunt Pony Club, for on each occasion they took the team title and fielded the winner of the Junior Individual Championship. The West Norfolk were supported and trained by Major and Mrs Derek Allhusen, whose great horse Lochinvar made a name for himself in the Three-Day Event.

In 1963 the West Norfolk, having won the Pony Club Show Jumping on the Wednesday, started the competition with confidence. The team consisted of Judith Garrard on Emperor Jones, Linda Garrard on Treeyews St Columba, Anthea Gow on Lucille and Patience Minister on Rosemary Allhusen's Japhet. They took the lead after the dressage, and in 2nd place was the Beaufort team, which included the two future winners of the Burghley Three-Day Event: Mark Phillips and Jane Bullen.

The cross-country course, designed and built by Geoff Chandler, started across the road from the Dairy Farm, took in the Maltings and the Trout Hatchery, and finished with the 'Road Works' at Capability's Cutting. The Trout Hatchery, with a knock-down post-and-rails on the edge, caused even greater problems than in a Three-Day Event, for it eliminated no less than seventeen competitors and put paid to the hopes of three teams.

Out of the nineteen teams that started, eight were eliminated. With three riders clear on the cross-country the West Norfolk widened their lead considerably, and the Duke of Buccleuch's, the only other team with three riders clear, moved into 2nd place. In the show jumping, held in the main ring, all three nominated West Norfolk members went clear, so the team scored a resounding victory from the Buccleuch. The Heythrop were 3rd and the Duke of Beaufort's 4th.

The individual honours went to Patience Minister riding Japhet, who had won the individual championship in 1960 when ridden by his owner Rosemary Allhusen. Henrietta van Bergen of the Garth Pony Club was 2nd; Judith Garrard was 3rd; and Jane Bullen on Our Nobby was 4th.

In the senior Championship Joanna Wheatley from the VWH won on Gay Romance; Mary Macdonell on Kilmacthomas was 2nd; and Barbara Pearson on Marlay Passport was 3rd.

In 1964 Linda Garrard and Anthea Gow again represented the West Norfolk. Japhet was ridden by William Boone, and Peggy Carey riding Shan was also a newcomer to the team.

Again the Allhusens' training prowess was plainly evident in the very high standard of dressage accomplished by their team. They established a convincing lead—and with only one pony penalised in the cross-country and none in the show jumping, they won the Championship by the very wide margin of 72 points. The Cheshire Hunt were 2nd, the Croome 3rd and the Beaufort again were 4th. The course was slightly easier than the previous year and out of twenty-two teams five were eliminated.

In the Junior Individual, Japhet won his third championship—an achievement made even more remarkable since William Boone, aged fourteen, was running a temperature and was heavily drugged. Later in the year Japhet paraded as one of the Personalities at the Horse of the Year Show where, ridden by Mrs Allhusen, he also won the Spillers Combined Training Championship for the second successive year. Linda Garrard was 2nd on Treeyews St Columba, and Jane Bullen with Our Nobby moved up

William Boone on Rosemary Allhusen's Japhet, Junior Individual Champions in 1964. Japhet also won the Championship in 1960, ridden by his owner, and in 1963 with Patience Minister.

The West Norfolk Pony Club Team, Champions from 1963 to 1965. In the photograph, taken in 1964, are (left to right) Judith Garrard and Emperor Jones, Linda Garrard and Treeyews St Columba, Anthea Gow and Lucille, William Boone and Japhet, Peggy Carey and Shan. With them are Major and Mrs Derek Allhusen, Mrs Rosemary Newton and Lady Alexandra Beaseley.

a place from the previous year. Anthea Gow was 4th, and Judy Bradwell, another future winner of the Three-Day Event, was 5th.

Judith Garrard won the Senior Championship on Emperor Jones—it was nearly a family double—and runners-up were Prudence Cawston and Charm, who a year later were to finish 6th in the Three-Day Event.

In 1965 twenty-two teams qualified and there were ninety-eight contestants for the Junior Individual Championship. There were some changes in the West Norfolk team. Japhet had been retired and William Boone was riding Treeyews St Columba, Linda Garrard was on Lotti, Peggy Carey was again riding Shan, and a newcomer was David Lyles on the oddly-named 'Animal'.

In the dressage the West Norfolk had to give way to the Southdown and the Bisley, but after the cross-country they regained their customary position. The Beaufort were close behind, and with only one fence between the two teams the show jumping was a cliff-hanger. The three West Norfolk members whose scores counted all jumped clear, so although all four of the Beaufort members had clear rounds they could not displace the reigning champions. The Bisley were 3rd and the Cheshire Hunt (North) were 4th.

Linda Garrard won the Junior Championship from Sheelagh Finn of the Bisley on Satinwood. Third was Richard Walker on Plucky Pasha, of whom Sir Andrew Horsbrugh-Porter writing in *The Field* remarked with some prescience: '. . . he looks big enough to have a go at Badminton one day'. Mark Phillips was 4th on Kookaburra II.

Angela Martin-Bird on Fulmer Featherweight, from the Crawley and Horsham Pony Club, won the Senior Championship from Fiona Pearson who had competed also in the Three-Day Event, finishing 12th on Tam O'Tullochan. In the Pony Club competition she was riding Ballinkele on whom she was later to have considerable success in senior horse trials.

When the World Championships came to Burghley in 1966 the Pony Club moved to a new venue at Cheltenham Racecourse—and it was here that the remarkable run of successes achieved by the West Norfolk came to an end.

Index

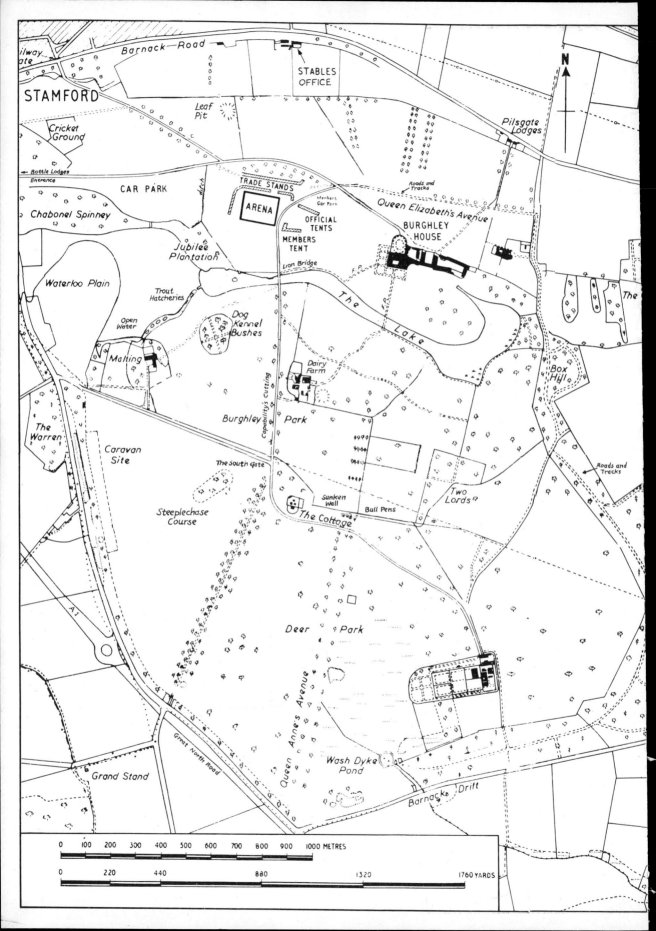